The Key To Loving Yourself

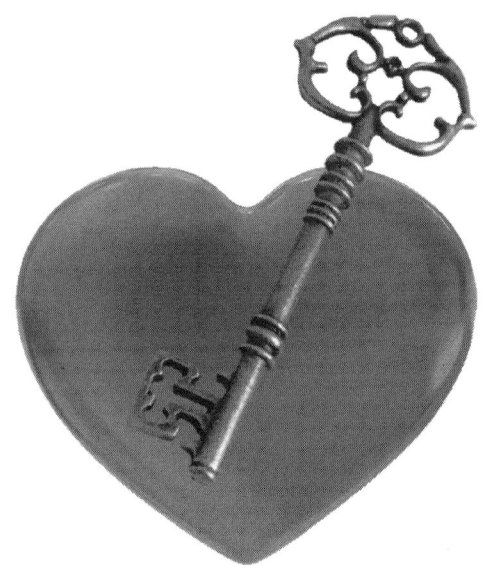

By Britta Hochkeppel

The Key To Loving Yourself
By Britta Hochkeppel

Copyright © 2014 by Britta Hochkeppel

All rights reserved. No part of this book may be reproduced by any mechanical, photographic, or electronic process, or in the form of a phonographic recording, nor may it be stored in a retrieval system, transmitted, or otherwise be copied for public or private use – other than for "fair use" as brief quotations embodied in articles and reviews without prior written permission of the publisher.

The author of this book does not dispense medical advice nor prescribe the use of any technique as a form of treatment for physical or medical problems without the advice of a physician, either directly or indirectly. The intent of the author is only to offer information of a general nature to help you in your quest for physical wellbeing and good health.

ISBN-13: 978-1503244689

Dedication

May this book help you find the initial spark deep within where you rediscover the part of you that is awake and listening, free of judgement and holds the key to your door to loving yourself.

Acknowledgements

My many clients, who taught me so much, encouraged and inspired me to put my ideas down on paper. My wonderful friends who have shown their loving support for my work and for all those who read this book.

Contents

Chapter 1	What is Life Force?	11
Chapter 2	Our Belief system	19
Chapter 3	Awareness	27
Chapter 4	Conscious thoughts	31
Chapter 5	Change your attitude	35
Chapter 6	The Present Moment	39
Chapter 7	Meditation	43
Chapter 8	Your Home	47
Chapter 9	Friends and Co	55
Chapter 10	Our Body	59
Chapter 11	A Meditation Technique	77
Chapter 12	Relationships	81
Chapter 13	Broken Heart	87
Chapter 14	Let go of the Past Letter	95
Chapter 15	Chair exercise	99
Chapter 16	Pillow bashing	103
Chapter 17	Attracting the Partner you want	105
Chapter 18	The Make Over	109
Chapter 19	Our Unseen Energy	117
Chapter 20	The Meaning of Disease	127
Chapter 21	My Cases	133
Chapter 22	My Relationship with Spirit	141
Chapter 23	My Unseen Friends	147
Chapter 24	My Story	161

Foreword

For many years I have been thinking about writing this book but the time was never right until now.

Working as a practising Naturopath-Kinesiologist but most importantly as an Energy-healer has enabled me to gather the much needed information, insight and knowledge that have inspired me to share my experiences with you.

I have come to the conclusion that we all own that unique fingerprint that might add up to just the right blend of information for one of the seekers out there, so here is my version.

In my experience of work in this field I have enjoyed many interesting encounters with clients and their stories, as I call them, which over recent years opened my eyes widely to the fact that by focussing on cleansing and healing the individuals body/mind/energy-balance and most of all, guiding them to re adjust their quality of thought, proved to be the best healing formula.

I believe that the quality of our thoughts create our life`s past, present and our future experiences, on all levels. Most of us still lack understanding and knowledge of the great importance of this fact and hold on to old belief systems, which claim that happiness and health, let alone success can never result from just thoughts.

However, everything within begins as an energy spark from a thought. We have the choice of its vibrational quality and therefore become director of its outcome.

Once we understand ourselves better and the power of positive mind, we can become co- creators of our own life, no matter how dark your past may have been. It's all about the quality of the energy within us, and how we project our belief system into our daily lives.

Chapter One
What is Life Force?

What is Life Force?
There are many different ways to describe it. Let's start with the term used by the ancient Chinese.

The ancient Chinese described it as 'Life Force'. They believed 'Qi' permeated and linked their surroundings together. They linked it to the flow of energy around and through the body, forming a cohesive and functioning unit.

The ancient Chinese believe that this energy current flows through a network of fine energy lines, called meridians. These work as a very individual and unique telephone-network for communication between body/mind and organs within our system.

When energy current shows signs of stagnation or blockage, the Chinese apply acupuncture amongst other techniques to reinstall a free flow of energy and balance.

The Chinese practise a lot of other energy balancing and enhancing techniques, Qi-gong Thai-Chi etc. that I wont, go into at this stage.

Quantum Physics
Energy information explained using science

We may consider every cell in the human body as a library of information. Each cell is made of molecules, each molecule is made of atoms, and each atom is made of electrons, neutrons and protons.

In connection with Einstein's familiar formula, E=mc2, we have been taught that matter and energy are equivalent. That we can convert energy into matter, and that the energy in a piece of matter is equal to the mass of the matter times the speed of light squared. While in the past it was believed that electrons were particles- matter existing at some point in space. Now, according to particle physics, electrons are not particles all of the times, but sometimes behave like waves of light. The current consensus is that they are both wave like and particle light as all is matter.

In fact, in the world of quantum physics, it seems these elementary "particles" (including electrons) don't really exist at all. What does exist are: relationships, correlations, and tendencies, to actualize from a multifaceted set of potentials.

At this level it is strikingly evident that there may be no objective physical reality at all. What the scientific community once thought was there in the sub atomic realm and what the educated world was taught to perceive as real simply does not exist. The new physics tell us that matter may actually be nothing more than a series of patterns out of focus and that sub atomic "particles" aren't really made up of energy, but simply ARE ENERGY!!

Niels Bohr, who is regarded as the father of quantum physics, pointed out that a particle only becomes a particle when we look at it. The new physics tells us that the observer cannot observe anything without changing what he sees. Moreover Princeton researchers Brenda I. Dunne and Robert G. Jahn have shown that this concept is not limited to the micro world of quantum interactions. Astonishingly they have through a series of well-documented experiments, established that our minds, our intent, *can* alter the outcome of events!

Long story short, this confirms that mind can change matter and certainly if the intention is of positive thought- quality, the positive energy current will create a positive echoing within our system. This fact may be of interest to all the critical minds out there.

What Happens if
The flow of 'Life-Force' is interrupted?

Most of us are born with a free flow of "Life-Force" energy current that runs freely through our body, providing our body-mind network with all the necessary vitamins, nutrients, very simply put, via our little soldiers, the cells.

What Happens if
We encounter damage to this flow?

Especially during our childhood, we may encounter some form of trauma or encounter a longer period of suffering, either through one event or an entire chain of events as we grow up. This sows the seed of energy stagnation. If ignored or left untreated this can develop from energy stagnation to a full block and result in disease and other physical imbalances.

Why?
Stress is caused by a variety of factors, but fear is the most predominant one.

It is the result of negative experiences of situations of the past, caused by a single event or an entire time period. Our body-mind system responds to stress by creating tension in the soft tissues, muscles, and organs.

This internalises the sensory and vibrational information of whatever causes the stress. Life Force is used to record this information in a special memory-matrix within our soft tissue. It is a bit as if we have a computer within.

If the stress is not wholly resolved, treated, acknowledged or released the life force remains held in this formation.

Due to the fact that the precious life force is trapped in a negative thought-loop, in time causes physical and emotional and psychological problems, because the energy that is being constantly used to maintain the stress symptoms is unavailable for present time or positive use.

The constant stress memory continually informs the body-mind system that something ill is going on. Subconsciously we keep up refreshing the past trauma on cellular level, as if it is still happening and integrate it into our daily life.

This leads to even more stress, miscommunication and a build up of the already created imbalance or it prevents us from healing and being able to move on from it.

The body tissue has cellular memory. It records pictures, sounds, smells, tastes and types of stimulation that were present during traumatic experiences or stressful periods in a person's life.

As mentioned previously, the body-mind system has to continuously exert energy to hold the stress and negative information loop within the tissue and structures.

Eventually a person's life becomes anchored into the stress system and increasingly exhausted and drained, because a huge part of their Life force energy is wasted or used up for incorrect thought upkeep.

Result of this will present itself on any level which ever levels were affected by traumatic event or time experienced and even though they try, it is difficult to change.

The symptom snowballs into an entire book of symptoms, which will need to be released and healed.

Chapter two
Our Belief system

Our Belief system

Suffering
Why do we suffer from what we experience?

Why does it not disappear in time, or we have an inbuilt mechanism that dissolves the negative memory? Why do we store it and spend a lifetime to punish and prove to ourselves that we are unworthy, or unlovable? Not good enough!

A model that I find interesting to use here-from Hawaiian shamanism and allied traditions -is that everyone has three inner selves: the Basic Self, the Conscious Self and the Higher Self. These 'selves' correspond to the subconscious, conscious and higher conscious, and also to body, mind and spirit. Each self is crucial in our life`s journey.

Very importantly the Basic Self includes our inner child, that living self within us which got stuck around the age of four to five. The inner child yearns for love and acceptance. It carries all our fears and inadequacies, our shame and guilt, need for approval, respect for authority, and feelings of powerlessness, as well as our spontaneity, sense of wonder and joie de vivre.

The Basic Self holds our childhood beliefs, messages and scripts, good and bad and clings to them tenaciously, unless we give it new instructions. As a growing child-energy, we are like sponges. Between the ages of three to six years in my experience we tend to absorb most of the core seeds of our closest environment, our parents, brothers, sisters, teachers and the media worldwide.

We continue to build our individual network of what we accept as our truth and create our life from these belief-systems.

Here comes the sad part. Unfortunately most of mankind lives under a negative and fearful mind concept, which does not allow positivity or creativity of any shape or form to unfold easily.

Our parents are mirrors of their gained negative belief system and will project these onto us. They too are victim of their own upbringing. However, this does not help us, the growing child being brainwashed by the following negative belief systems.

*"You`re **no good** at spelling"*

*"**No good** with numbers"*

*"**Not good** at art"*

"You`re too thin"

*"**No good** at sports"*

*"**Not** talented"*

*"You`re **too fat**"*

*"Don`t **trust** anyone"*

"Rich people are bad"

"Money is evil"

"You will never be anything special"

"Life is a struggle"

Growing up under these circumstances it is a miracle that some of us are able to free ourselves from this negativity. However most of us cannot.

In addition to the negative thought feeding, we encounter additional trauma. For example: the loss of a family member, suffering sexual abuse, or being bullied etc.

The toxic combination of a negative belief system and experience of trauma is the ideal seed to continue to attract further negative experiences to confirm and mirror to us, that we are unlovable and undeserving.

This develops into a solid belief system and sinks into our **"Basic Self"**. This in return attracts new and further negative thoughts and especially all the experiences we need to confirm that we are what think we have become

. For example: the girl who suffered sexual abuse as a child is likely to attract abusive partners or relationships where possibly her first, second and third partner all mistreat her, act disrespectful towards her, confirming her feelings of being unworthy and unlovable.

Most people do not understand the underlying reason for this or can explain to her why she keeps on attracting these wrong and negative males into her life.

Stripped of all emotions and looking at this purely from a spiritual-energy angle, what has happened here is the female re creates the negative experience and proof that she is undeserving and lacks self-love etc. All of this is not meant to sound light hearted. I am using this purely as an example for understanding.

Whether we like it or not, we all are *energy* beings. How are we meant to grow and be healthy and creative, if we lack positive energy brain food, are starved of love, receive no warmth? This is like waiting for a plant to grow in a dark room, without sunlight or adding water!

So many out there are unhappy right now, feeling isolated and displaced in their profession, hating what they do, or where they are in life, who they have chosen as their life partner. The children do not show him/her respect or acknowledge his/her constant emotional effort and sacrifice given on a daily basis. This results in a very negative thought system and the question: "How did I get here?"

Maybe because what your heart desired was not good enough, not safe enough you became the accountant instead of the astrologer, (nothing against accountants) the nail technician instead of the interior designer.
We settle or marry the wrong partner, because we fear being on our own and believe that we will never find the right partner for us anyway.

We give up on ourselves, fall asleep and drop into a coma - state of mind that prevents us to live the life we were intended to live. Instead we turn into that plant, rot away in the dark room, and accept that as our truth and our reality!
If we continue to refuse to look at this and we deny our selves the right to be happy, to experience true love, radiant health, and to be wealthy, we certainly stay there until we die. What a waste of time.

During all of this, our body develops the earlier mentioned energy blocks, which result from our experienced trauma and negative belief system.

Even worse than running on half empty, most of us add to the physical loss of vitality and energy, by continuously stuffing it with a huge amount of unhealthy foods and fluid-toxins whilst we are forever chasing time.

It is very depressing, to observe this self-destruct attitude, which is usually accompanied with all the suitable excuses, our ego creates, to keep it all up.

We are asleep, disconnected from ourselves. We will not find our happiness, fulfilment if we stay in this state of mind.

Chapter Three
Awareness

Awareness

What to do? Wake up!
The first step is AWARENESS

When we have some patterns buried deeply within us, we must become aware of them in order to start the healing process.

Perhaps we begin to mention the condition, or see it in other people, perhaps we attract help, thanks to our higher self always trying to surface, and maybe we attract a teacher or healer, a course.

Whatever it is, give it a try.

Often our reaction to this first and very important stage is to think that it is silly, a waste of time, what`s the point? Perhaps it doesn`t make sense to our way of thinking, we may find it unacceptable, we don't want to do it. Our resistance comes up very strong. We may even feel angry about it.

Actually, such a reaction is good, if we can understand that it is the first step in our healing process.

It is only our fear of change or to face the inner shadows, what you must understand here is that:

YOU are the co - creator of your life, your experiences.

YOU CAN heal your life, your mind is your healer!

Get used to the fact that you are an energy being and therefore need to apply techniques to raise these energy levels.

Let's look at a few ways to raise and improve your inner vibrations and energy. It has been proven that applying positive thought affirmation continuously for three weeks will nullify the negative vibration thought.

Chapter Four
Conscious Thoughts

Conscious Thoughts

Here are some ideas to raise your vibration
Become conscious of your thoughts

Everything that you think about will at some stage manifest into your reality!

Believe it or not, we do choose our thoughts. We may habitually think the same thought over and over so it does not seem we are choosing the thought. But we did make the original choice. We can refuse to think certain thoughts. Be honest and look how often you have refused to think a positive thought of yourself. Of course you can also refuse to think a negative thought of yourself but it seems to me that everyone whom I know or have worked with is suffering self-hatred and guilt to one degree or another.

For example, if you are predominantly thinking: *"I never have enough money to pay my bills"* you will always struggle, or *"I am not good enough"* - but for whom exactly?

You need to understand that thinking and living low energy thought form can only attract further low vibration. This is why awareness is so important. Once you gain awareness, your brain will flag or make you notice where your quality of conversation is going, for example:

In the midst of saying something to one of your teenage children that was intended to make her/him feel ashamed of his/her conduct, you stop and remind yourself that there is no remedy in condemnation.

Instead you shift the energy of conversation into a more loving and understanding form. This shift raised the energy in a split second and will only result in a positive response, even if not in that instant. Once started, keep it up and apply your awareness, almost like a warning system, to notify you when you are being negative towards yourself, for example the inner dialogue...my bottom is too big.... my eyes look tired.... I hate my fat stomach...I hate my cellulite...I don't like my boss...etc.

Instead, try saying to yourself. *"I am filled with love and affection"* Find something you like about yourself and highlight it - yes, there will be something you like, maybe the colour of your eyes, or shape of your nose, the colour or texture of your hair, your smile etc.

The more you replace a low energy thought with a high energy thought, even the oldest and toughest negative thought is nullified by the positive vibration, again energy. All you have to do is persevere!

Don't you owe that to yourself? Or do you want to continue bullying your inner child? What is the point of that?

Whatever happened to you in your past, even more a reason and actually your duty as the parent of your own inner child to now begin to nurture it and flood it with love.

After all the greatest love of all is learning to love yourself. If we don't love ourselves we will not love others or attract true love. We will attract a reflection of our ego - which is never a good idea really, as our ego connects its value to what we have achieved on a material level and is never truly satisfied.

We have to understand and see our ego as if it is that naughty child, mostly trying to get our attention, feeling under the constant threat of loosing the competition to be better, more beautiful and wealthier than everyone else around us - exhausting don't you agree?

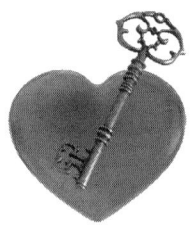

Chapter Five
Change Your Attitude Towards Your Past

Change Your Attitude Towards Your Past

Yes, most of us have got a few stories to tell. You maybe grew up in that dysfunctional family, were bullied at school, experienced wins and losses, ups and downs.

As time goes by we tend to re create the past events in a more colourful and dramatic way, and add negativity to it, to use it for us as an excuse to continue struggling in our lives.

This happens on the sub conscious level.

We often stay in a state of blame towards one of our parents or siblings or the main perpetrator of our experienced misery.

What we have to realise here is that this way we will never move forward or heal from any of those experiences.

How can a bird be free in a cage?

Again, it is our awareness that helps us to recognise that maybe forgiving or finding a way to let go and heal is much more what our inner child needs.

First of all we need to understand that our parents were victims of their circumstances and then projected their negative belief system onto us.

A different way of looking at this
Going back to our spiritual pathway

I am a strong believer that before we incarnate onto the planet, we chose the time, but we also choose our parents. We choose our sex, the country and the journey and then we will look for the particular set of parents who will mirror the pattern we are bringing in to work on in this lifetime.

Then, when we grow up we point our fingers accusingly at our parents and say: you did this to me, or I can't do this because of you.

Yes, the truth hurts sometimes. We are here for learning and evolving in our energy and spirit. The body is a tool, an important vessel to get us through our life path. When we have reached our learning destination for this life the body vessel dissolves but our energy stays, very simply said.

We need to understand we are an endless evolving and learning energy being that constantly connects and corresponds with other energies. I believe knowing and understanding this gives a greater and deeper sense of what is life all about and why am I here?

Allow the past to be in the past as it serves you not anymore in the present moment or for the future.

Place the past in a big pot and stick a lid on it and allow it to rest. Only extract the memories and information that will provide you with positive or creative tools. Everything else needs to be spiritually binned.

Chapter Six
The Present Moment

The Present Moment
Your Power is always in the Present Moment

All the events and situations you have experienced in your lifetime up to this point have been created by your thought system and belief system you have held in the past.

They are creation of your thoughts, words you used yesterday, last week, month and years.

What is of importance in this moment is what you choose to think right now. You might want to pause for a moment and make yourself aware what thought you are thinking at this moment? Is it negative or positive?

And do you want this thought to be creating your future? No matter what the problem was or is our experiences are just outer effects of inner thoughts.

It really makes no difference how long you have had a negative pattern. Change the thought and the feeling will go. The point of power is in the present moment.

How amazing is that? You can begin to be free in this moment.

Enhancing the moment

For a moment, I would like you to become aware of your surroundings. Even if the room appears familiar, look around you as if you are seeing it for the first time.

Really look. Take in the designs, textures, colours and shapes. Can you feel the magic of this moment?

*What can you **sense** right now*

*The **sensation**, of your clothes against your skin*

*People **chatting** in the background*

*A clock **ticking***

*A car passing by or **traffic** noise*

*The sound of **birds** singing*

*Can you feel the **magic***

*What can you **smell** right now*

*What can you **hear** right now*

Can you feel the sensation of simply being alive right now

This little exercise helps your brain to connect to reality and the moment which helps to distract from our constant memory link either to the past or fear of the future and it trains your mind to bring a heightened form of awareness into your daily life and you can expand this by repeating this several times during your day.

When you do ask yourself, how am I feeling right now? Am I feeling good?

Chapter Seven
Meditation

Meditation
Make Meditation regular practise in your life

Even if it is only for a few moments each day, this practise is vital. Let me give you a few brief insights on the basics of meditation. Most of the people I see still believe that one has to sit in the lotus folded position and chant mantras, well let me enlighten you that there are many different ways to meditate.

Origin
From the Far East

Most meditative techniques have come to the west from eastern religious practises particularly in India, China and Japan and they are over 5000 years old! The primary purpose of meditation has been religious although its health benefits have long been recognised.
Studies have found that regular meditation increases longevity and most importantly the quality of life.

Benefits
What else does regular meditation improve?

- It reduces anxiety

- It reduces high blood pressure

- It improves the oxygen levels in the blood cells and rest of tissues

- It reduces serum cholesterol

- It strengthens and calms the mind

Introduction to meditation

Position: Sit in a comfortable chair.

Clothing: Wear comfortable clothing, or open buttons and belt if they prove too tight.

Posture: Sit upright in the chair – but relaxed. Your feet are placed (hip wide) apart and the soles of your feet are fully touching the ground.

Do not cross your legs or bottom of your legs, as you will block the energy flow!

Place your hands into your lap – let your shoulders drop
The hands during this exercise are gently placed resting on your thighs with your palms facing upwards.

Now allow yourself to let go. Take a few deep breaths and allow the head stuff to dissolve, don't think, just be.

Begin to count backwards from 100 – 1, slowly and allow any intrusive thoughts to come and go, like waves of the ocean. Pay no attention to them.

When you have reached 1, you can gently open your eyes stretch and continue by adding a brief grounding technique.

(To enhance this technique simply add 100 each time you sit to meditate lengthening the time, say from 200 – 1, etc.)

After each meditation, it is of importance to make sure that you are grounded, here my advice:

Standing up – making sure you are standing feet firmly on the floor, close your eyes surround yourself in a bubble of golden light and imagine you have roots coming out of the soles of your feet.

Plant the roots deep down, deep into the earth. The body needs to sway to ground, allow this to develop for a minute or so, then open your eyes and continue with your day.

Chapter Eight
Your Home

Your Home
Mirroring your state of mind

Did you know that the home you live in mirrors your state of mind quality as well as the quality of thought of its previous owners? Your home has no choice but to absorb all your energies and thought waves that you and every occupant within those walls releases 24/7! Scary!

It cannot run away or collapse under the burden that sometimes oozes off its owners constant negative inner dialogues. It matters not if these are created by spoken words or just in inner negative dialogue.

Energy is energy, never trapped or confined by a vessel. It evaporates literally into our space.

Over the past few years, I have been called out by various individuals to perform energy healing for: properties, work spaces and offices, due to the fact that some properties were so overloaded with negative energy-thought vibration.

This had a draining effect on each individual living there, or working there, which meant that the owners became unwell or their business stagnated. Nothing improved no matter what they did.

Unless you can sense or see energy like myself you will stay unaware until the symptoms become clearer.

So let's look into what you can do, which would help to cleanse your space and enhance a positive vibration that will match your newfound positive thought quality.

Go and stand in your entrance hall, if you have one. Look around you, what do you see? Is it cluttered, dark, stuffy?
What feeling do you get, each day when you turn your key to enter your home? Is it a sense of comfort and relief, a safe return to your nest? Or is it a sensation of inner tightening in your centre of your stomach? Please be aware that these vibrations pass in split seconds, but I am sure you know what I mean.

You will have at some stage walked into a space that resonated with you in balance and gave you a sense of warmth or comfort. Or maybe for some unknown reason you felt very uncomfortable and somewhat cold and unwelcomed.

Either way, it is energy that you can feel - just because most of us choose not to pay attention to it does not mean that its not there all the time, mirroring our energy right back at us!

Energy is just as present as the rainbow colours that appear, if we hold a prism into the sunlight. Just because we can`t see the entire colour spectrum of the light, does not mean that it is not there.

The entire atmosphere is filled with visible and invisible light and energy waves.

Become aware of the energy that your home environment reflects back at you. Paintings, colour of your walls, plants, books, magazines, how you arrange your furniture all create energy into which you are catapulted for at least half your waking life.

While this may seem silly or absurd, I urge you to become open minded, which is the intention of my book. You need to realise that the more in balance you are on all levels the better your life quality will be. This is fact! It is your choice.

High-energy surroundings
Strengthen your entire body-mind system

The ancient Chinese art of *feng shui* has been with us for thousands of years and is a gift from our ancestors. It describes ways to increase the energy field of our home and workplace.

Suggestion's to improve your home

- Look into the basics of feng shui for your home; it is fun and not expensive

- Keep it clean

- Make sure fresh air can circulate

- Surround yourself with colours that resonate with you

- If you have favourite colours, make sure you do not paint all four walls but maybe one feature wall only!

DECLUTTER!

Very important, anything that is stale, for example dried flowers, a heap of older magazines, clothes that may have been thrown onto the floor, pick them up. Dust the areas such as: shelves, dressers, cupboards and don't forget your houseplants. Wipe them down with a soft cotton cloth and make sure they are healthy and cared for (plants respond strongly to positive energy).

Give your home a good deep cleanse whilst playing happy music or classical music (that has been proven to have the most balancing effect on brain waves and surroundings).

Or play something current that you love, which makes you smile from within, maybe sing along to it whilst cleaning. Your home will love this and absorb all the positive changes.

When you have finished, drizzle some peppermint oil drops or lemon grass oil on a few areas that will not stain, and enjoy that aroma. With a bit of creativity and love you can change almost any space into a brighter and lighter energy. Enjoy this experience!

Music
Become aware of the music you listen to

Harsh, pounding, musical vibrations and especially the lyrics of hate, pain, anguish and fear and violence are low energies sending weakening messages to your subconscious and infiltrate your life with similar attractor energies. If you want to attract violence, then listen to the lyrics of violence and make violent music part of your life.

However, if you want to attract peace and love, then listen to higher musical vibrations and lyrics that reflect your desire.

Television
Become aware of the television you watch

In my opinion the majority of television shows, provide a steady stream of low energy most of the time.

Children in America see 12,000 simulated murders in their living room before their 14th birthday!

Television news place a heavy emphasis on bringing the bad and ugly and in my opinion selected and chosen information, which may not always be the truth but what we are meant to accept as our truth.

It`s constant stream of negativity that invades your living space and attracts more of the same into your life.

You see it is the same concept everywhere. Once you become aware, you have the choice to select what you want to see. Maybe choose more comedy, or documentaries, which may bring to your attention the desperate state our planet is in and inspire you to do something positive for the planet or a friend in need.

Have you noticed that as well as the endless feed of negativity displayed by TV programmes, drug cartels use the commercial breaks to tell us that happiness is found in their pills etc.

Yet another illusion and lie, as your life quality will never improve by suppressing symptoms of negativity and popping that pill instead. The entire concept I feel is wrong.

Unfortunately, most of us are unaware and offer ourselves gladly for our daily entertainment and *'unwinding TV-evening'* to absorb even more negativity and depleting mind food.

Lovely, and then we are surprised if we have sleep disorders. How can an overactive and negative mind, starved from health, positivity and creativity be at ease and able to switch off?

Chapter Nine
Friends & Co

Friends & Co
Gaining more awareness

As you are now gaining more awareness, sit back for a moment and think about the people you have around; the individuals that you call your friends.

What is the overall energy of your friends? Positive? Creative? Or is it negative or stagnant?

Do you remember when you and your best friend would often share similar problem stories and go through it together, especially when you were teenagers? But if one would unexpectedly come out on the other side, then suddenly your best friend appeared different and somehow not the same or the relationship was not as good as before, or estranged.

As we age and I am sure you have noticed this around you, if we are slightly struggling in our daily life and sharing our negative thoughts with others, who then can feel sorry for us or attempt to be the good friend or support and at the end of our conversation we both agree that things will get better in time. Well, if we then suddenly prove a positive change is beginning to manifest, for example a better job maybe, or more money or we have lost those extra pounds in weight and have begun to do regular exercise often you will notice that your positive changes, are the seed to creating a mild threat to the majority.

Instead of sharing your happiness, the ones who feel threatened, will find a way to drift apart from you, and avoid you, because now they sense a separation of the energy bubble.

What was a shared negative is now just left with them and highlights too clearly where their areas of weakness lies and as a human race we somehow prefer to be stuck in a negative thought system and we hate change - especially positive changes. It is too uncomfortable; our ego has too much fear of change.

A true friend will share each stage with us, free of attempt to project negativity, nor will he/she avoid or drift away from us, just because we are becoming too happy or healthy. It is often better to have two real friends then lots of low energy ones. It also works the other way round.

You can raise your own energy levels by being in an energy field of others who resonate higher energy. So be conscious of being in the presence of and interacting with higher-energy people. Anger, depression, hate and fear will melt away the more often you share their positive energy.

We are all mirrors of our inner thought qualities both to us and also towards the relationships/friends that we hold close to our hearts during our life journey. We can learn a lot from just observing and listening with an open heart, instead of being overcritical or fearful.

To let our friend unfold how they want to and just be there for them, through thick and thin, because we want to be there, not to gain points, which we then expect to be rewarded for at a later stage - that would be low energy thinking!

The less we involve our ego and the more we connect to our higher self and our heart, the better. Instead be kind and understanding and stay open minded.

Chapter Ten
Our Body

Our Body

The body like everything else in life is a mirror of our inner thoughts and beliefs.

Every cell within our body responds to every single thought you think and every word you speak *Scary...I know.*

Continuous negative thinking and speaking produces imbalances in the body and can lead to diseases.

A face riddled with downward facing features is definitely a mirror for negative thought system overload.

Our constant negative inner dialogue will create a mental pattern, which will create illness in the body in time.

Remember I mentioned energy called life force running through our system. This life force energy depends on our inner thought quality.

Everything is connected, constantly talking to each other on many levels simultaneously.

Once you truly understand the concept of energy and positive thought, you will want to enhance it as much as possible.

Here a short version list, from head to foot which might prove helpful in building awareness as an overview, how certain areas of our body resonate with our mental patterns. See if you can relate to some of them, either from past experiences or maybe even something more current.

I have offered suggestions under each section.

Head
The head area is associated with "us" anything imbalanced in this region is a sign for us to pay attention:

Suggestion
Stop judging yourself constantly and let go.

Headache
Conflict or indecision, often wanting to do one thing but feeling you should do another. Very critical about the self - "what have I done wrong?"

Suggestion
Forgive yourself and let go, stop trying to be perfect at everything, relax.

Migraine
Conflict, suppressed resentment, perfectionism

Suggestion
Ask yourself what is it I am suppressing? Let go

Eyes
Always connects us with our version of how we see the world we are in.

- Short sighted-not looking ahead enough, not seeing things in perspective.

- Long sighted, living in the future, ignoring details.

- Glaucoma-feeling under pressure, suppressing all emotions.

Suggestion
Face your truth, see what is happening in your world and choose to be open for change if needed. Relax and learn to trust.

Sinus
Problems represent being irritated by someone close in your life.

Suggestion
Maybe, it is time to communicate in honesty and stay in your own power, create peace and harmony in your life.

Ears
Ears represent the capacity to hear. When there are problems with the ears, it usually means something is going on that you don`t want to hear.

Suggestion
Ask yourself *"what is it that I do not want to hear?"* Or *"what is painful for me to hear?"* Accept what you receive and write it down, and then communicate with people involved.

Tinnitus
Tinnitus can be a symptom of the level of tension and not listening to your inner voice or inner guidance.

Suggestion
Begin to listen to your gut instinct. You cannot ignore the inner voice forever.

Try it and see what happens.

Sensitive ears
Reacting to maybe too many harsh and negative words being expressed around individual.

Suggestion
Communicate with the person(s) who is using too much negativity.

Throat
Stands for expressing our self, our voice, our need to be heard. Creativity. Speaking up for who we are.

Suggestion
Learn to express your truth on several levels and live your life how you would like to, by introducing creative aspects that may have been suppressed before.

Sore throat
Indicates anger, if we lose our voice too it means we are so angry, we cannot speak.

Suggestion
Write down what makes you angry or what you find frustrating and when your voice has returned, communicate that with the people involved.

Tonsillitis and Thyroid problems
Represent frustrated creativity because we feel we cannot do or be who and or what we want to be.

Suggestion
Become aware of your resistance to change or where you are blocking your creative energy to emerge and why you are either doing this or allowing others to take away your power.

Let go!

Shoulders
What are the burdens you are carrying? Are you carrying others worries or responsibilities?

Suggestion
Let go of what is not yours to carry.

Breasts
Femininity, nurturing, mothering

Suggestion
Express your femininity in a healthy and balanced way, allow yourself to have a rest; even Mother Teresa needed a break!

Heart
The heart is the centre of Love, giving as well as receiving.

Suggestion
It is never a good thing if we have closed off our heart to life or love, no matter what or how bad the experience.

This will result in the heart literally shrivelling and it becomes cold. As a result the blood gets sluggish and we create the path to heart conditions, for example angina, and heart attacks.

You have to learn to forgive; even a broken, shattered heart can heal if you allow it. There is always a new dawn. Practise acts of kindness even when you are hurting the most and the Universe will echo this kindness with sending you the healing help you need, never in the way you expect, so stay open.

Lungs

Suppressed tears, grief, feeling you have no right to breathe, feeling unworthy, overprotected, blockages about giving and receiving

Suggestion

Let go of fear, allow yourself to take life in. You have the right to live your life fully.

Start today by practising yoga breathing exercises that focus on opening and expanding the chest

Go dancing or running, whatever it is you enjoy and can do on a physical level that creates joy, maybe put on your favourite song and dance.

Stomach

It digests all the new ideas and experiences we have. When we have stomach problems it usually means that we don't know how to assimilate the new experience. What or who can't you stomach? What gets you in the gut? Do you suffer constipation? Are you clinging to the past? Are you holding back emotions? What is it you are holding on to? Why do you refuse to give yourself pleasure in your daily life? Are you overworking?

If you suffer diarrhoea, why are you not allowing yourself to be nourished? Learn to trust the process of life.

Irritable Bowell Syndrome (IBS)

Refusing to eliminate and refusing to be nourished at the same time, the colon represents our ability to let go - so try to begin today.

Suggestion

Awareness - Take in the information in healthy bites, and allow it to settle. You need not know it all, nor let go of all at once. Relax and practise deep breathing exercises and eating healthy and slowly will also help here. Have up to eight glasses of bottled or pure water per day.

Relaxing exercises and meditation will be very helpful for you. If you ignore the signs your stomach problem might develop into an ulcer, always pay attention and listen to your body. Let go of fear.

The Back

Our support system

- Problem in the upper back-lack of emotional support, holding back love.

- Problem in the middle back-guilt, feeling stuck in a situation, can`t let go.

- Problem in the lower back, fear of money, or the lack of, lack of financial support, feeling alone.

Suggestion

Begin to trust the process of life. Read self -help literature, which will help you gain awareness and a way to start positive mind work. Release the past and begin to focus on how to love and nurture yourself.

Practise, exercise, and enhance the flexibility and strength in your spine. Yoga, swimming, gymnastics will help too. Take small steps and enjoy the process. Important – it is always the combination of exercise and practising positive thinking techniques.

Genitals

Genitals represent us, who we are, and how comfortable we feel and fit in our role as a man, or a woman.

It represents the most masculine part of the masculine principle and the most feminine aspect of the feminine concept.

Every organ in our body is magnificent and beautiful and perfectly natural. However, when it comes to sexual organs, we often seem to hide away from expressing our self in a natural way or even naming our sexual organ in its original way.

A lot of this still resonates from our past.
If we have experienced trauma on a sexual level, or observe parents and people in the media behaving in a negative way, towards the topic and what it is, we gather the belief system that it is something *"dirty"*, something we must not, or cannot express.

A balanced sex life is very healthy and very natural; whatever feels right for you and your partner of course. If you have chosen a partner whose sexual appetite is fulfilled with sexual intercourse once a week, but your sexual appetite is higher, say 10 times per week, you will have a problem.

Suggestion
Always communicate in truth with your partner. Try and find a compromise that works for both. If Love is part of this relationship you will find ways.

Cystitis
Feeling extremely irritated (especially with your partner)

Suggestion
Drink plenty of herbal teas, place hot water bottle between your legs, and communicate with your partner what it is that is troubling you.
Let go of anger.

Vaginitis
Usually means feeling romantically hurt by a partner.

Suggestion
Let go of self-blame or hate or feelings of failure, or resentment towards the partner, for this will just prolong the inflammation - let it go.

Prostate problems
Represents the self worth and also the belief system, as he gets older that he is not man enough or losing his original masculinity.

Suggestion
Accept this new phase, eat healthy foods, and practise exercise in small and healthy doses. Trust the process of life and know you are exactly the same man you were 20 years ago, just wiser!

Legs

Mobility. Our legs carry us forward in life. Leg problems often indicate fear of moving forward or we are holding back on a certain level because we fear change or the unknown. Are you going in the direction you want to?

Suggestion

Work on enhancing your confidence, so face your fears and remove them one by one. For strengthening: go dancing. Another good way to exercise your strengthen legs is fast walking surrounded in nature.

Knees

Knees like our neck have to do with flexibility, only they express bending and pride, ego and stubbornness.

Often we would like to move forward, but we do not want to change our ways or we are fearful, that we will lose something precious along the way therefore we become stiff in our joints.

I also feel knees are very much linked to our surrender to the flow of life. If we resist they persist. Knees take a longer time, to respond to healing as do shoulder and neck issues because of our ego strongly being involved here, and the ego is like a naughty child always creating blocks for our higher self.

Suggestion

Learn to let go of what it is that you are afraid of losing. Let go of trying to be in control. Life is about movement.
Surrender to the Universe and try out new things.

Meditation techniques, Thai -chi, yoga, swimming, dancing will be helpful here.

Feet

Our feet represent staying grounded, security and survival, stepping into the future, but also in connection to our past-present-and future.

As we age sometimes we lose our confidence because we have allowed others to take it away or maybe because we are on our own and feel more vulnerable to continue our journey, so we get wobbly and unsteady on our feet.

Suggestion

Feet love to be massaged so go and try reflexology massage. This is very stimulating and detoxing on many levels and a great start in shifting the old stuff.

Feet also love walking naked on sand or grass and dancing. Good footwear is also important, maybe less of the killer heels and maybe more of the sensible shoe for the walks in between!

I have only touched these main areas for now, as it is meant to give you a taster for insight and hopefully inspire you to change if some of the areas mentioned are causing you problems.

Body language
Learning to Love your Body

In my observation mainly working with female clients over the last years, I have witnessed just how cruel we are with ourselves and our bodies, whether it is its size, colour of skin, type of skin, colour of our hair, texture of our hair, nose, lips, eyes, teeth, breasts, stomach, hips, legs, knees, feet forgive me if I have left something out! Ladies

On average, our morning starts with floods of internal verbal abuse in the bathroom, it happens so fast and subconscious that we do no longer pay much attention to it, however our basic self and inner child are always listening to all the abuse almost nonstop! Shocking

We choose certain areas in our physical appearance that we study in an obsessive, self-destructive manner; ready to stab into our flesh with our internal verbal butchers knife.

We microscopically highlight all the areas with our inner negative magnifying glass all whilst brushing our teeth for example saying: *"oh dear, my ugly eyes have bags underneath"* or *"those ugly hips have got even wider"*, *"my stomach is so fat"*, *"I won`t fit into anything"*, *"my nose is too big, I wish I could afford a nose job"*, *"I am so ugly"* while we wash and cream our self or apply our make-up, getting ready for another day.

By the time we leave the bathroom we have made sure that we feel unattractive or ugly and all the inner negative, magnified areas of all our bad bits are now even bigger. We are convinced that everyone else out there sees us the same way and must think we are unattractive or ugly too!

And not just ugly, we, as a person are unlovable and so on.
THANK GOD this is in our mind only, luckily people see us as a whole person and not just our highlighted "ugly bits"...that 'awful' large nose or 'huge' buttocks- that they do not look at us with judgemental eyes.

It is just us, who practise relentless inner verbal torture and bully ourselves, most of the day, every day. For me it is a miracle that our bodies continue to function at all.

What a waste of energy, don't you agree ladies?

If we do not change or heal nor improve our relationship towards our self, in time we will develop physical manifestations that can result in disease of serious nature.

It has been scientifically confirmed that the continuous negative inner dialog starves the chosen hated body zone, which means that the cells transport less oxygen and vitamins and minerals into those areas.

The metabolism almost slows down by 50% in and around those areas, and in time, that part of the body, will be less nourished and only deplete more, so thoughts like: *"I hate my hips so much"*, will only create more stagnation of fatty tissue to settle around the hip area.

With the quantity of negative and depleting thought- forms staying in the hip area, they can`t change, all they can do is stay the same or increase because YOU are telling them to by subconsciously giving them the command and starving your physical, emotional and mental body from the much needed love frequency it needs instead to begin to change.

So the most important first step to take is to STOP the verbal abuse!

1) Make yourself aware which areas you dislike or even hate.

2) Write down your reasons why you dislike/hate those areas and when it began.

3) Who was the first person in your life that made you aware, that something apparently was not right with you the way you look?

4) You may have to revisit your childhood.

5) Who are you comparing yourself with?

6) For who exactly are you not good enough?

If one of the reasons is that some of your inner negative dialogue results from being bullied at school or a sibling, or other, the very next question is *why have you continued to bully yourself?*

Please know, your inner child has to observe your thought dialogue from within and is forced to listen to your words, without the possibility to escape.

Those of you who have your own children, surely you avoid telling your son/daughter that he/she is ugly or fat, or that their nose is too large, their eyes too small, their stomach too fat etc.

Instead you see your child through the eyes of love and in all its uniqueness, which is how it should be. You would be mortified, if you witnessed someone constantly giving your beloved child negative, deeply upsetting and depleting verbal input all day or most of the day.

So why do it to yourself? You too were once that child that now depends on the love and nurturing thoughts you will feed it with. Don`t starve yourself any longer of loving yourself.

As I am sure if that is what you would feed your growing child with, it probably will not stay happy or healthy for long. It would not develop an interest or experience joy, it certainly would not go outside much, being so ugly, but hideaway and be deeply saddened and probably feel very unloved and unworthy.

Instead, write a list of all the things that make you unique, everything that you love about yourself.

Begin a positive dialogue with that "hip" or what- ever area and say to it: *"I love you exactly as you are"*.
This is of upmost importance as before the body/ mind level is able to begin to change or heal, we need to accept it as it is and begin to send love into it as it is.

Chapter Eleven
Meditation

A Meditation Technique
For Enhancing Loving Yourself

"The Loving light-meditation"

Sit down in a comfortable chair or armchair. Make sure that all mobile phones are banned from the room, so you will not be disturbed. If you like and it helps you to relax, put some relaxing music on, if you prefer silence, that is fine too.

If you have never practised meditation do not be alarmed, you do not have to be an expert in visualising. Just relax and be open to accept what you see or sense. If you are wearing tight or restrictive clothing (buttons, belts) now is the time do undo them for the time being - just don`t forget to do them up afterwards!

Sit down; take a deep breath, nice and slow, eight repeats, deep breath in and slow breath out. Each time as you exhale I want you to allow your thoughts to roll around your head on the in breath and dissolve on the out breath, allowing yourself to relax deeper and deeper with each repeat.

Feel how you are beginning to sink into your chair just that little bit more. Let go for the moment just be.

Nothing matters for the moment this is your time.

As you relax, make yourself aware of the soles of your feet touching the ground firmly and allow yourself to become nice and heavy, allowing your body to let go of any tension, it may be holding on to. Take a deep breath in and a slow breath out. Now I would like you to direct the insides of your palms to face each other as if you were going to hold an invisible balloon, and stay approx. 10 inches apart.

Continue to stay relaxed, and very gently make yourself aware of a subtle current that radiates from the inside from one palm to the other. If you do not sense anything, just focus on the warmth radiating from the inner palms, for a moment. Whatever you feel or sense is ok just go with it.

Now I would like you to imagine that this invisible balloon is a bubble of white light and in its centre appears subtle colour of pink.

Now you hold the white ball of light with its pink core in between your palms.

I now want you to focus on one part of your body you dislike the most.

Gently place both your hands, with the ball of light on to the area and imagine that light drenching the unloved area with love. To enhance this feeling you can think of someone or something you love and which creates that subtle warm fuzzy feeling, just for a split second. Now move your hands to the area.

You might sense a very slight sensation of warmth or soothing nature. As you do this, say to yourself: *"I love you and accept you unconditionally and completely."*

Please, repeat this 3 times, each time focusing first on creating the white light energy with the pink light in its centre, before placing or resting your hands on the area of concern.

In addition you can send the loving light into your body by placing the hands over your heart area or thymus gland, and repeating the sentence: " I love you completely and unconditionally."

Then slowly come out of the meditation and make yourself aware of the room you are in and when you are ready gently open your eyes. Stretch out your limbs and notice a subtle change.

This meditation takes 10 minutes; the more often you do it the better. Try once a day for 3 weeks, or continue as a daily ritual, no side effects guaranteed.

Watch the positive changes appear in time, be patient and kind to yourself.

Chapter Twelve
Relationships

Relationships

It seems all of life is about relationships. We have relationships with absolutely everything!

The relationships with people in your life reflect the relationship you have within yourself. The relationship you have with yourself is highly influenced by the relationships you had with the adults around you as a child.

You even have a relationship with food, which some of you might recognise, connected to positive memories around certain food preferences or comfort foods. This is only a comfort food to you because of how your emotional mind has stored the eating experience, including the smell and taste, accompanied by the atmosphere of maybe security or laughter.

Equally, you will also be aware of imbalances caused in relationships with food. For example if you are an emotional eater or over compensate with foods in vast quantity, or need to get up at night time to soothe your system with a preference for sugary foods, this too is a result of whatever you experienced around the subject of food and how your parents influenced you during your development.

The inner dialogue that you would use for praise or telling yourself off will be very similar to the words that were used around you and said to you by your parents. I am not listing this to point a finger or blame parents. We are all victims of victims.

Relationships are mirrors of us. As mentioned earlier in my book, what we attract always mirrors either qualities we have, or beliefs we have about relationships.

Unfortunately, most of us do not realise how much the state of: our belief system, our childhood experiences, and observation of the quality of the love relationship between our parents, will influence and eventually decide what type of partner we will attract into our lives.

If we do not find a way to get to know who we are or heal certain imbalances within, our belief system prior to entering a love relationship we will find that the mirror we have attracted will bring with it many bitter pills to swallow and a recipe for heartache."

For a moment think about someone who you might have close around you, for example a friend who is undependable and lets you down, then look within.

Learn to become aware of the mirror working here.
Mirrors are placed for your inner growth, not to destroy you. You just need to see them with your wise inner eye, rather than your ego eye.

The questions you ought to be asking yourself

- Where in your life are *you* undependable?

- When do you let others down?

- What, in your opinion, would happen if *you* let others down?

Are you afraid they might not love you as much? Is it fear of rejection, if you let someone down? The more honest you are with your findings and feelings, the quicker and better and deeper the healing result.

It is all about learning, without judging yourself. We are all in the same class room, each one with different topics; however love is the most important lesson that most of us need and one must truly understand and accept that without love, nothing will grow, nothing will heal.

"If you do not love yourself you cannot give love."

Everything in this Universe revolves around love. Animals that exist deprived of love will become dark and aggressive and bite or hide away. A child growing up without love will never feel loved, and will stay dependant on exterior response, for example praise and material wealth will be of priority. He/she will develop into an individual that will measure his/her values with the rise and fall of his/her achievements and will most probably attract a partner, who will confirm this belief system.

Yes wealth is a fantastic energy, but it can't buy back time or love. If you have a lover that is cold and seems unloving, look to see if there is a belief system within you that came from watching your parents in childhood that says, love is cold. Perhaps, you observed emotional or even physical abuse?

Or, was your father strict, never easy to please, leaving you with the feeling whatever you did was never good enough?
Or a mother, who was too weak, never stood up for herself and allowed everyone to walk over her? I could list hundreds of stories all revolving around subject of love.

If the energy 'Love' is allowed to flow freely within our system it can truly create such incredible force, that will nourish us with its unique warmth, strength, inner light, happiness, kindness, beauty, creativity, ability to overcome any obstacle, and fear of any hardship.

If we experience a learning lesson in matters of 'Love' it can also act as an energy force that will yank us into the darkest and most lonely isolated place within our soul, and should we find our healing, which most of us hopefully will, you will emerge with a new found quality of love in your heart.

Learning to loving yourself is the most important lesson in our life journey!

Chapter Thirteen
Broken Heart

Broken Heart

Break up - Anyone who has experienced a separation, a loss of something or someone you loved dearly, knows how intense the impact can be on the entire being.

It is almost as if we are infested by a deadly virus that zaps our entire energy and drains us of any thoughts of positivity and life force. The stages of a broken heart are mainly experienced as follows, but of course it may vary individually.

Shock - we have just been told or have found proof of what we may have feared the most. He or she does not love us anymore and wants to end the relationship. We experience rapid heartbeat, hot and cold sweats, we may feel sick and feel faint. Adrenals are responsible for the shaking or trembling of our entire body. Everything within our system is now reacting as if we are in a shock situation, which could equally have been created by an accident or other trauma of great intensity.

Our mind is trying to make sense of the words heard and attempts to find an answer or a solution. It develops a combination of panic and confused inner chatter and a deep sense of helplessness and fear.

Grief - floods of sadness will follow, hours or even days after the initial shock. The body/mind level tries to shed as much of this painful and depleting energy as possible. There are only so many hours in the day and crying for several hours will leave you feeling drained and exhausted which will demand your body to fall asleep eventually, allowing your body to regain strength to face the next day.

The stage of crying is a very important release and should not be suppressed, as it will only manifest into other shadows for you to deal with in the future. Try and go with the flow but also allow yourself to do nice things for yourself, even in those dark moments.

Numbness - we transition into the stage of numbness and total loss of energy due to our life force having withdrawn into our deepest aspects of our being, which is for our own protection and energy reserve to be saved for us to keep us going.

Mentally, we are entering a phase where our being seems as if cocooned by a veil, and energy cloud that helps us to disconnect and experience less intensity of pain, due to lack of clarity and exhaustion.

Whatever tasks we need to fulfil in our daily life during this time we seem to manage somehow on autopilot and use the nights to continue the painful detox of a broken heart.

Anger - gradually emerging out of the state of numbness and autopilot existence, we experience a new emotional brain wave, which is represented by the energy of anger.

Anger is a very useful tool, because it produces a lot of adrenalin and a short-term boost of vitality, which is desperately needed for our next phase that we are about to enter.

We are now creating the seeds of our new life, without our partner and if children are involved in this life lesson, you need all the energy that you can get.

Be careful that you do not lose yourself in creating a stage of resentment, as this emotion energy will only deplete your system and will not have any effect on the one who left you.
Even in the moments of us feeling angry and possibly resentful at our partner for putting us through mental/emotional torture, we need to be witness to the higher lesson experienced here.

Honesty is very important in your healing process. Go within and ask yourself.

Maybe we were not as happy as we thought or hoped we were? Maybe what we thought was love was our fear of moving forward or our fear of change? Did we really love each other? How much did we really have in common? Have we been living separate lives but under the same roof? Somehow the universe will find a way to separate what does not belong together whether we like and accept this or not.

Time will reveal answers and we will find a new quality of life and clarity and gain greater insight. Why we no longer suit our partner, or maybe never did but never had the courage to face the truth. In my observation this clarity appears between two to three years after a separation.

I am talking about the broken heart created by separation, not the loss of a loved one through death caused by illness or accident.

The broken heart created by this type of trauma can take longer, however the stages seem to be experienced in similar order.

Help to heal a broken heart
Gradually emerging from the experience, leaves most of us feeling vulnerable, unsure of who we are and what we want, and if we can ever trust again.

We lose our confidence, certain aspects of our personality, maybe feel unattractive and are busy creating new negative belief systems. We feel as if we have left soul fragments behind and feel lost.

If you have learnt anything by your experience then please understand that every lesson is presented to you for your growth and improvement.

I know this is hard to digest but it is the truth.
I also believe you have suffered enough, during the learning process, wouldn't you agree? Now is the time, for reconnecting and reuniting with yourself.

START TO LOVE YOURSELF.

I have gathered a few tips, which might prove helpful to you.

The Reality-check
Ladies and gentlemen, there is a time for grieving and hurting, reflecting and turning within and then there comes the time that we need to exit the shadows and emerge again.

Nicely said, we are now in the stage of transformation from the caterpillar to the butterfly. We need to make new choices. Why not use this time to reconnect to your truth, to who you really want to be; to focus on what you really want and begin a new true and loving relationship with yourself.

If you do not change and heal your inner aspects, nothing will change for you -it can`t.

The exterior world in all its glory can only reflect and echo what you are sending out. Accept this and begin your transformation.

Remember irrespective of what`s happened during your life so far, it is very important that you recognise that you already are an amazing human being.

Fact! You are that very unique and precious link to the whole world. The world would not be the same without your energy being part of it, whether you think it or not, whether you feel it or not.

It is what it is. You were born to feel joyful and enjoy the magic of life. You have been blessed with the gift of life.

You were born to live a purposeful life, overflowing with all the things you could possibly wish for.

We all have the inbuilt birthright to live and experience love and wealth and happiness in abundance, we just need to become aware of our door blockers.

It is YOU who is your worst enemy. It is YOU who is your worst critic. It is YOU who is your co-creator, the designer of your life.

It is the law of the universe, the law of attraction.

Focus on what you want
Life is now. Now is all there is and your priority attention should be how can I 'support' myself?

What is it you want to come into your life? Begin to write down your wishes on a piece of paper and stay aware of what quality of thoughts you are thinking whilst writing down your wishes.

If you hear words of doubt or an inner nagging voice, tell it...OUT!

For example, let's imagine, even though your heart has been broken, you can be broken hearted with an open heart.

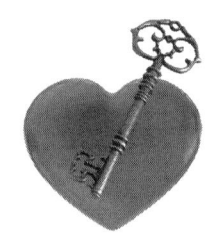

Chapter Fourteen
Let Go of The Past Letter

The Letting go letter

We all have residual thoughts and words or conversations we may not have had the chance to share with our x partner but we need to get it out of our system, otherwise it stays and depletes our energy.

One way of doing an emotional detox is to sit down and write him or her letter designed in a way of conversation. Make sure you will not be disturbed during this process. Take an A4 paper and begin to tune in. The order is not of importance, more so it`s content and how you connect emotionally to each topic.

For example: go back to a hurtful scene in your memory and as I always say either write it down or write it off... Reconnect to that moment and allow yourself to become emotional - the more the better.

For example:
Dear (name)*"remember how mean and hurtful your words were towards me? "You were cruel and broke my heart"*, etc.

There may be many different incidents - do not do them in one go - spread this exercise over several days. The more detail the better. When you have written enough and feel 'lighter' you can take the letter and tear it up. The residual paper scraps you can now place in a bowl that is fire resistant.

Go outside when you feel it is the right moment and set light to the paper left over.

While you watch it burn and shrivel to ash, I want you to say in your mind: *"I set you free but most of all I am setting myself free and allow my heart to be healed."* It is ok to get tearful - this is good. Always allow your emotions to emerge. It is all part of the healing process.

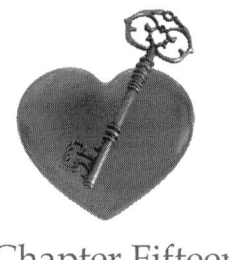

Chapter Fifteen
The Chair Exercise

The Chair exercise

Another helpful exercise is to have that conversation; even though the person you need to have this conversation with is no longer present. You can and should allow your anger and residual pain to come out. This is a very powerful and amazing release and my favourite.

Find a room where you will not be disturbed.
No phones etc. Now take a photo of the person you want to have that 'conversation' with and place it on the chair where you can see it. If you can visualise him or her please do that.

The fact that they are not physically present does not influence the effectiveness, as they will receive the energy shift via energy on their spiritual level. Often I have experienced when people have applied this exercise the person who the 'conversation' was directed at, hours or a few days after, either rang or somehow the Universe showed signs of recognition, I think this is worth a mention.

Back to the chair -Now I want you to begin to shout at the person who gave you the grief

Go for it! Shout or even scream at him or her - everything that really hurt you or made you angry. Everything, that caused you hardship or heartache.

Let go, don`t worry how loud you are. If you are connecting you will get very emotional. Allow this to happen. When you feel empty, you will know when to stop. You may revisit this exercise whenever you need to should you need to repeat it.

After this exercise you will feel exhausted or tired and need to have a little rest, or a cup of tea.

Be very proud, for you have just been witness to a very powerful and deep release. It takes true courage to face these exercises. Well done.

Chapter Sixteen
Pillow Bashing

Pillow Bashing
*Anger and resentment must be released from your
system, because they are very depleting and harmful to your health.*

In addition should you be experiencing days where certain areas of your body ache or burn or show physical signs of manifestation of emotion - usually anger or grief - please take two pillows and start bashing them against each other whilst screaming or shouting; *"I am so angry!" "I am hurting so much!"*

If you own a pillow that could take physical abuse, please apply this exercise. You will find that your pains will most of the time either disappear or reduce strongly in their level of intensity.

Best thing to aim for is to forgive. Forgive yourself and forgive your partner - but only after you have made use of the exercise with the chair!

All these rituals assist you greatly in leaving your hurtful past behind and help heal your broken heart from within. Now that you are gradually beginning to feel more like a person again, why not sit down and create a list of your ideal partner? It may be a while until you feel like making use of the next exercise, but whenever you are ready, there is no rush.

What type of partner would you like to attract into your life? The more detailed the better. Be truthful in your wish list, as your inner self will know when you are dishonest and ignore it.

Chapter Seventeen
Attracting Your Partner

Attracting Your Partner
Finding your ideal partner

Before you begin this exercise free your mind of any doubts and try to see it as a game. It is very important to work with the new you that is free from judgement and doubt and negative thought remember?

Sit down in a comfortable chair with a clipboard and A4 paper.

Ok here we go, I have written out a few points, which might stimulate your wish list:

Example: *height, size, fitness level, sense of humour, kind, wealthy, grounded, love of nature, looks after him/herself, loves to cook, is a good dancer, enjoys conversation, is romantic, is intelligent, is open minded, likes to read, likes to travel etc.*

Ask whatever it is you wish him or her to be. When you have finished, sit back and close your eyes. Visualise, what he or she looks like, feels like. See yourself totally fulfilled with this partner.

Imagine yourself together with this partner. What tone of voice do they have? Or what type of laughter? What is their energy like? Trust your insights. You do not have to be a psychic to own a healthy sense of intuition and it is your intuition, which will grow volume in its voice the more you practise this type of exercise.

When you feel you have had enough of your visualisation, open your eyes and feel happy and relieved to have had this experience and know this is what you will attract in time. Pretend you already know them. Pretend they already are in your life. Yes it takes practise, but it is a nice exercise and I know it works!

Giving out what you want to attract
Be what it is your are seeking

Once you have formed a specific picture in your mind of the person you want to attract into your life-space, and you know how you want them to treat you and what they will be like, you must be what it is you are seeking. You can't have a desire to attract a mate who is confident, generous, non-judgmental, and gentle, and expect that desire to be manifested if you are thinking and acting in a non confident, selfish, arrogant or judgemental ways.

If any of the low energy vibration qualities are still part of your thought world you need to let it go.

Please know, the right person will show up precisely when you need them (no, not when your ego decides) and when you are able to match up. You must be that which you desire. When you are, you attract by radiating it outward.

This is fact!

Sometimes we think we are ready for that new love to come into our life, but are we really? It is very important to distinguish between our ego talking or our basic child-self which craves attention or diverts from our own healing process because we do not want to deal with it.

We might be too lazy to change. In general we like to resist change. Are you really willing to allow a new person into our life? Have you healed from your previous relationship and have you been able to let it go? Or will you compare the new person with the previous one?

In any transformation it is very important that you are honest with yourself, I keep repeating this. Honesty is the only way forward.

Chapter Eighteen
The Maker-Over

The Make-Over

Replace your current negative thoughts with positive ones. Say "Yes" to change!

If there are aspects in your life that you don't like for goodness sake do not give them even more energy by thinking about them. You need to focus on what you want and attract that into your life.

All that mental energy you waste on complaining about your circumstances is a magnet for attracting more of that. Change your inner speech to what you intend your new circumstances to be.

Your thought: *"I can't stand looking in the mirror, because I am so out of shape.*

"Your positive thought replacement or affirmation is: *"I allow myself to let go of anything that is not love."*

You could choose a photo of yourself where you approve of your shape, or someone who you would aspire to look like and stick it onto your bathroom mirror and use it as an additional support for visualising your new shape. Every time you go into the bathroom to brush your teeth or do other things you can gaze with joy at this image, which represents the future you, and look forward to wearing new clothes and the feeling of vitality that will come with it.

Your brain cannot differ between reality and imagination, so it pretty much absorbs everything we feed it with. Imagine that your consciousness is two miles long, but your sub consciousness is 20 miles long.

It is the repetition of your thoughts that create your brains skills and abilities as it learns and expands the entire time. It is you also who decides and judges the information coming in, either to be accepted as your truth or untruth.

That is why most exercises need to be repeated, remember when you were a child you would have needed to repeat tying those shoe laces, or how to balance on a bike or learning to write, to read, anything new needs repetition until your computer the brain has absorbed it and created a web-network order that makes sense for all the necessary pieces of its learning and development stage.

Our thought processes are similar only that we need not necessarily add a dance step physically when we create a new positive affirmation to nullify a negative thought pattern.

However I am sure if you created a dance in connection with your new positive thoughts it might go even deeper and flow better, because we are experiencing joy as we learn.

Everything flows much better, when we are adding laughter to it.

And your brain loves to absorb information and learning. It is an amazing learning muscle.

Make room for the new
Another important aspect of attracting what you want is to make room for the new to enter.

A little earlier I wrote about the importance of your home and the energy flow within your space.

You need to change your environment and adapt it to your new way of positive thought processing.

Your transformation needs to manifest and it can do that even better if you support yourself on a material level as well.

De clutter
In the recovery and healing stage after a separation you need to remove items that link you to that person if there is a negative thought pattern attached.

I am not saying buy yourself a new kitchen or living room interior what I mean is clean out your closet. Get rid of all the stuff you have not used for the last six months or so.

Clutter, represents a cluttered mind and does not resonate with the "new you". Clutter is the old sad and stagnant you.

The Universe loves positive rituals and symbolic gestures and it will make you feel a lot better within yourself, when you practice them.

When I de clutter I listen to my favourite music and maybe even sing along to it. I love to de- clutter and give to others the belongings I do not need. It is a positive ritual and the Source is always listening and observing.

Make small and affordable changes in your home, maybe move furniture to a new position, get some insight on 'Feng-shui' and follow the rules of what is the best energy flow for your home.
It will all reflect positive vibes to your energy and create a lovely balance and improve your health too.

Your Body
With the new you also comes the need to do something to wake up your physical balance.

A brisk walk in fresh air works wonders on a regular basis when depressed, or if your mind is suffering overload and you need to air the cobwebs. Return to do regular exercise of what you used to enjoy, and do it in a small dose to start with for several weeks, until you gain more physical strength. If you have developed any serious physical ailments in your past and you can`t do exercise, a short walk can be done most of the time.

Or try something new; Yoga is very good for reconnecting to yourself or body- balance, dancing, swimming or cycling. Maybe search for a walking group on the Internet or ask around if there are friends who would walk with you, to get you out again if you do not want to walk on your own. Or begin with a new hobby, maybe art, or singing or learning to play an instrument, do some acting in a theatre group or join a cooking class or baking class.
These are all very healthy activities that link the left and right hemisphere of your brain together and this creates balance and joy. This is what you want in abundance.

Nutrition
Clean out your refrigerator. Get rid of all those bits wrapped in foil.

Revisit your current diet. If you are eating too many biscuits or chocolate or any other processed food instead of wholesome foods, now is the time for change.

Remember you are doing this for yourself only. This is not about sacrifice, this is to set you free once and for all from any food addictions that you may be carrying around with you, which are feeding or linking with the negative thought pattern that you are trying to shift

Sugary foods and processed foods, too much alcohol and cigarettes are all crutches we cling to because we feel that without these things we could not live or do not want to. They are mostly linked to unhealthy emotions and unhealthy thought patterns. In addition, overeating on sugary foods and processed foods will have a direct influence on your chemical household within your brain and other organs, due to the sugar balance and imbalance, spiking up fast, only then to come crashing down.

The intake of too much alcohol will have a very negative effect on your brain, and mood swings, so if you are feeling depressed and crave all those drinks to numb your thoughts, think again, they will only pull you down even further the following day plus create imbalances within the chemicals released by your brain in attempt to bring back serotonin and dopamine etc. The result is that you will feel even less self worth, so best accept that alcohol is a dysfunctional remedy and acts more as a self-destruct mechanism.

If you do not wish to remove it from your life completely, you can still strongly reduce the intake frequency and amounts. With drinking my suggestion is to always order a big bottle of bottled water and drink this alongside your wine or other drink of your choice and slow down. Stop rushing the drink down.

You can live without it, if you want to.
The choice is yours.

Take deep breaths, relax and observe your environment. Alcohol is a nasty habit, if consumed uncontrollably. Too many out there are on a self-destruct mission, all under the lie of *"this is fun,"* *"this is how I relax* - all excuses. I know you don`t like to hear this, but it is true.

You are relaxed anyway, and, or, have to find a healthier option to create a more relaxed mind-set and not rely on your liver and kidney to detox it all for you. Most people are anxious and nervous, fear crowds or people and feel that *with* the intake of alcohol - they just don`t want to admit to it.
The choice is yours.

Information on healthy foods and lifestyle are available in vast amount, as well as literature on vegetable and fruit juicing or blending, which you can also introduce one day a week or replace one meal in your day which will help shed that excess weight. Furthermore it will support your recovery process with vitamins and minerals that help to detox your organs and help your brain and the quality of your thoughts too.

Everything is linked, our organs, our mind, our physicality, our emotion, our spirit and soul. Eating a healthy diet and a healthy intake of fluid, eight glasses of water (bottled) per day and less toxic drink helps our mind and body become or stay balanced. Regular exercise and regular mind relaxation, for example meditation, will in time provide you with everything you need and our life can change for good.
You deserve a good, healthy and happy life!
Open your arms and say; *"I am open to all the good and abundance in the Universe."*

Chapter Nineteen
Our Unseen Energy

Our Unseen Energy
The "subtle" energy bodies

The people of ancient cultures knew and understood that beyond its physical form the human body is a pulsing, dynamic field of energy. Through observation they developed an understanding of these basic and fundamental subtle-energies that surround and permeate the human form.

In Sanskrit this subtle-energy field is called kosas (body sheaths) while in modern and complementary medicine it is known as the bio magnetic energy field or Aura.

The Aura
The word Aura comes from the Greek word avra, meaning breeze. It looks like a luminous egg of pulsing, moving, dynamic energy that surrounds and interpenetrates the physical body.

The Aura consists of seven levels that correlate to the seven master chakras. These levels begin with the seen, the physical body, the etheric aura, and progress to more subtle and refined vibrations as we go further away from the physical.

The Aura looks a little bit like an onion with layers of luminous light.

All Auras are different and change constantly, as our thoughts, moods, environment and state of health change. Apart from moving around us, it acts as a shield of protection.

Auric damage and depletion is caused by: ill health, negative thought patterns, environmental pollutants, electronic magnetic radiation (mobile phones and computers especially), bad dietary patterns, addictive substances, stress or poor breathing techniques. It can be repaired by holistic healers, which is one of the healing techniques I offer or with the correct use of crystals and gemstones and supported with meditation.

I have the ability to see, read and interpret your emotional Aura and your core Aura, which helps me a great deal, in my field of work, to detect and rebalance my client's ailments.
People are opening up much more to the fact of accepting that there is more to us than meets the physical eye, which helps a great deal. Our Auric field is under constant bombardment and I am always surprised how much this subtle energy field can take before breaking apart into 'Auric' holes.

You will not necessarily feel anything when this occurs unless you are very sensitive and know your body very well and also have insight to this subtle energy body. What will happen in time is that you will experience a sensation of being burnt out or a presence of tiredness that just will not shift.

Yes it could be a sign for exhausted adrenals too or other physical imbalances, but often it is your Aura needing help to close the holes. If left untreated, this will lead to physical ailments and disease.

Having your Aura repaired is a very pleasant experience and I have not yet experienced anyone not feeling a noticeable difference afterwards.

Maybe give it a try.

Chakras

Chakras are funnel- shaped energy vortexes of multi-coloured light. The word chakra comes from the Sanskrit and means 'wheel' or 'disc'. Chakras are vitally important for your physical health, emotional wellbeing and spiritual growth.

Each master chakra has a linkage point associated with specific organs and endocrine glands. They must always be seen as a complete integrated system that works holistically. Chakras can also be viewed as step-down transformers for higher-frequency subtle energy and convert it into chemical, hormonal and cellular changes in the body. Each chakra vibrates at a different vibrational frequency and on a different note.

The major chakras

The **Root-chakra** is located at the base of your spine.
Spiritual aspect: Self- Awareness as a Human Being
Basic Need: Security, Confidence
Related Emotions: Fear and Courage
Endocrine Gland: Adrenal (Cortisone)
Associated Organs: Kidney, Bladder, Rectum, Vertebral Column, Hips
Colour: Red

The **Sacral-chakra** is located in your lower Abdomen
Spiritual Aspect: Self -Respect
Basic Need: Creativity within Relationships
Related Emotion: Possessiveness, Sharing
Endocrine Glands: Ovaries and Testes
Associated Organs: Uterus, Large Bowel, Prostate, Ovaries, and Testes
Colour: Orange

The **Solar-plexus** chakra
Position: Epigastrium, Below the Ribs
Basic Need: Valuing the Needs of the Self
Related Emotions: Anger, Resentment, Unworthiness, Guilt
Endocrine Gland: Pancreas
Associated Organs: Liver, Spleen, Stomach, Small Intestine
Colour: Yellow

The **Heart-chakra**
Position: Centre of Chest
Spiritual Aspect: Self-Love
Basic Need: To Give and Take Unconditionally
Related Emotions: Joy, Hurt, and Bitterness
Endocrine Gland: Thymus
Related Organs: Heart, Breasts
Colour: Green and often pink in its centre

The **Throat-chakra**
Position: Throat
Spiritual Aspect: Self – Expression
Basic Need: Ability to Accept Change
Related Emotions: Frustration, Freedom
Endocrine Gland: Thyroid Gland
Associated Organs: Ling, Throat, Intestines
Colour: Blue

The **Third eye-chakra**
Position: Forehead
Spiritual Aspect: Self – Responsibility
Basic Need: Vision and Balance
Related Emotions: Confusion and clarity
Endocrine Gland; Pituitary
Associated Organs: Eyes, Lower Head, Sinuses
Colour: Indigo

The **Crown-chakra**
Position: Top of Head
Spiritual Aspect: Self – Consciousness
Basic Need: Acceptance
Related Emotions: Despair and Peace
Endocrine Gland: Pineal
Associated Organs: Brain
Colour: Violet / Purple / White

Another subtle energy network is represented by an internal communication centre, which corresponds amongst you thoughts, organs and energy lines, called **Meridians**.

Meridians
Life Force

In Chinese and Ayurvedic medicine, health is seen as the fluent and harmonious movement of energies at subtle levels. This energy has various names. The Indian yogis call it prana, as do Ayurvedic practitioners. Ayurveda is the traditional holistic healing system of the Indian subcontinent.

To Tibetan lamas it is called langom, while it is known as sakia- tundra or to the followers of Shinto (the indigenous religion of Japan).

The Chinese call it chi or qi. Loosely translated, all these terms mean life energy or as described earlier as 'Life force'.

Life energy is considered to have clearly distinct and established pathways, definite direction of flow, and characteristic behaviour as well defined as any other circulatory system in the physical body, such as blood and the vascular system. In the Chinese traditional medicine, these pathways are the meridians through which 'Chi' flows.

The meridian theory arose from thousands of years of medical practise in China. The word meridian came into the English language through a French translation of the Chinese term jiing-luo, which means to go through, or a thread in a fabric, luo means something that connects or attaches, or a net.

The Chinese, in acupuncture, developed the use of needles to unlock these pathways. In Shiatsu, the Japanese use direct thumb and finger pressure on acupuncture meridians points (acupressure points) to achieve similar results. Through increased awareness of meridians one can practise crystal therapy more effectively, as meridians provide profound insight into the disease pathway and are therefore a most useful diagnostic therapy tool.

So you see, everything is connected and depends on each other and staying balanced on all levels - physical level, mental level, and the emotional level.
Summary of all this is attempt to enhance your awareness and to realise, that although a lot of those energies are invisible, they nevertheless exist and need you to be good to yourself, especially in the quality of your thought patterns.

Crystal energy

Crystals and gemstones work holistically through resonance, using subtle-energies. By applying this subtle-energy resonance in a coherent, focused way to dysfunctional energy systems, they restore stability and balance.

Crystal healing thus allows you to reconnect with your natural harmony by stimulating your body's inherent healing mechanisms and increasing the flow of your 'life-force'. This results in the releasing of dis-ease bringing restructuring and alignment.

Obviously there can be physical causes for illness, but not everyone exposed to a particular virus or bacterium develops the illness.

Healing is a uniquely personal process. If we listen to our bodies and learn to understand their language and their messages, we become increasingly aware of the connections between body, mind and spirit.

You may be ignoring your body's messages, not because you intend or want to, but because you are simply unaware of them amid the pressures of modern living. Most people react to illness by trying to eliminate the symptoms as quickly as possible with direct conventional medical intervention.

There is nothing wrong in seeking relief from unpleasant or distressing symptoms, but if you want your body to be dis-ease free, you will also need to understand why you are ill. Remember, we are complex beings. You are your co-creator.

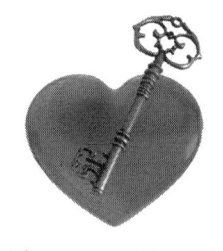

Chapter Twenty
The Meaning of Disease

The meaning of Disease

If we accept that everything comes from the One Source, then disease itself must be part of the Greater Plan rather than a mishap or act of punishing us.

In my experience, looking at disease in a psycho spiritual way is just another manifestation for soul growth. Conscious awareness of the experience can enhance the healing process as long as the consciousness does not remain purely in the head. Every call of the body needs to become aware of the changes that are taking place and to release old patterns and habitual behaviour.

In most cases dis-ease or disharmony appears in the mind before it appears in the body.

We can all choose how we want to deal with it, however if we ignore the mental and emotional aspects or suppress them, they will return and in other or additional areas of our body, also varying in intensity of its level of pain until we have 'learnt' our lesson and are ready to move on. We all seem to obey pain, so pain is our greatest healer in one way.

Meditation Exercise

In my quest to find the best exercises for you, I discovered this one a few years ago, which to this day I love and apply a lot.

Anyone who has tried this visualisation exercise has had great insight and found it to be very helpful in the healing process. Before you do this Meditation please read it through first, as with all the other exercises, and then sit down to do it.

Meeting your Illness

(Stepping into The Magic written by Gill Edwards)

Relax deeply then imagine that you are in a forest.
Don`t worry if you can`t see it you may sense it. Go with whatever it is your mind allows you to experience at this stage. We worry too much going into any type of new way of working or accessing our mind and spend more time blocking or doubting the information we are actually meant to be receiving, which in most cases would actually help a great deal.

Let`s return to the meditation-visualisation.
Sit back comfortably and imagine you are in a forest. It is a moonlit night, and trees are silhouetted against the silvery light.

In your mind`s eye, open your inner eyes now and see the forest around you. Hear the Owls hooting, and feel the whispering breeze. Now look for a path opening up in front of you and begin to follow this path which leads deep into the forest, stepping over fallen tree- trunks, pushing low branches out of the way, hearing the crunch of your steps on the leaves underfoot (you can see deer or anything else you choose to allow to appear).

In the heart of the forest, you come upon a grassy clearing, brightly lit by the moon. You settle down in the centre of the clearing and wait (you may see or sense some animals gathering around or behind you).

Mentally you ask for your illness (past or present) to come to you. It may take the form of a person, a creature or an object, or you might simply sense a presence (very important here is that you MUST accept what you see or sense. Do not question or try to explain rationally as that will stop it from happening).

Wait for your illness to join you in the clearing. When it arrives, greet it as a friend, Say that you are glad to see it, since you have to learn from it. Tell it that you know it has (or had) an important message for you, and that you are eager to understand this message for you. Ask your illness what it came to teach you. Then wait patiently for its answer, which might come as a word or words that you hear, as thoughts, as images, symbols or memories.

Make sure that you are clear about what action you need to take and ask the illness if it will leave you, if you take this action. If not, what else do you need to do? Know that all the answers are within you. You created the illness, you know what it means and you know how to heal it.

Fact! You simply need to access your inner wisdom. Remember to thank your illness for its message. Ask for the healing to begin today and continue during the coming days, weeks, and months if necessary. Picture yourself healthy. Feel your body regaining health and vitality (maybe use a memory of your childhood where you felt an abundance of vitality or joy).

Then gently bring yourself back into the room. When you have done this correctly you will be surprised at the accuracy and maybe also the emotions that arise during
or after.

Please allow yourself to experience this and let go.

You don't need to do this meditation often, but it is worth doing when you feel stuck in your physical pain or if you feel that your illness just is not shifting!

Chapter Twenty-one
My Cases

My Cases

My Healing - Practise
I feel a deep sense of gratitude and compassion for all my clients who have sought my advice or guidance and healing over the last years.

Without them I would not be where I am today, so I want to say a very big and warm thank you to you all, who have honoured me with your trust, your faith and your honesty. **I do love you all.**

Sharing a few stories

Let`s say, Mr Smith suffers from a bad knee, on his right side of his body and is experiencing constant pain, stiffness and has had several operations with no success and seeks my help. The key to unlock the 'blocked life- force' is to detect what is Mr Smith`s underlying emotional-spiritual - body-message he is not understanding?

To detect the information I need, I use a combined technique of reading his energy and connecting to him on a psychic level, deep into what I call the core energy. Once I connect to the core I get a sense combined with a story told by the body. This is a unique and fascinating experience for me and each story is different. Even when the same person returns for a follow up treatment we receive further information or something new that is now ready to emerge.

I receive a variety of images, key words that often come directly from the part of the body where the pain has manifested.

Every cell in your body has a cellular memory, in which it stores all what you are and all what you have experienced, especially the emotional trauma and physical trauma.

I discovered when Mr Smith was a young man he viewed the world and the people around him in a very black and white manner, in attempt to hide and to protect his vulnerability and sensitivity, resulting from experiencing a somewhat emotionally cold childhood, and him never being good enough for his father.

During teenage years he manifested a belief- system, which made him believe that if he shut off and pretended to be hard and tough it would protect him of his true feelings and his fear of not being good enough, his main focus was to suppress his true feelings. In addition whenever he experienced a threat to his belief system or was surprised by sudden changes he would create resistance to the change and turn away if necessary and act against his core truth.

Knees represent flexibility but also pride and ego, if reacting in a negative way. The fact that his right knee was the painful and rigid one proved that the threat he experienced was against his masculine principles, because the right side of the body represents the male concept and everything that goes with the masculine concept.

If he could have understood his body language at an earlier stage he would have maybe sought help or read some self help literature or found a therapist before his knee cracked under the emotional overload. Maybe he would have found a way to let go of the suppressed emotions and his fear and his knee would have improved with a combination of emotional release work and physical exercise.
His knee did improve and we were able to relieve him of long-term backache and other joint pains.

It's never too late to begin with the healing process.

A lady, who came to me, suffered from lower backache, which was reducing her life quality so much, that this was the reason why she came. Again, pain is the voice we hear. She is a passionate golf player and was now unable to enjoy this hobby due to the increase of the crippling pain

The core problem here was her belief system that she does not deserve happiness at this stage of her life, as she always worked very hard and only recently allowed herself to reduce her working hours. Sometimes we become workaholics so we can distract ourselves from our true emotions that want to be looked at and maybe release.

As I dived into her past further we had to look into her childhood, which was this time lacking love and warmth from both parent energies. Although she thought she had released her anger and resentment towards her parents, she had not let go of some aspects of low self esteem which is very often the result of abuse, be it physical or emotional, or just a cold parental upbringing.

Everyone is unique and some may grow under those circumstances but others break and loose themselves.
All can be healed you just need to be open. After we were able to release some of her residual issues, her back healed within three sessions and she now enjoys her favourite hobby 'Golf' and has added several more creative new hobbies into her life. Her entire energy has transformed and she radiates with a deep glow.

A particularly interesting case was presented to me at my early stage of my healing- practise in 1998, when I was still in Germany. At that time the majority of Germans did not understand or tolerate anything linked or associated with paranormal activity.

This initial encounter connected me to the ability that I now use every day on every client and my lesson was to trust it.

When one works with the 'invisible energy' as I like to refer to it one has an ability to connect to information that we today translate as being 'psychic' or 'intuitive.

Working as a Naturopath, which is what I was and still am, one had to be very careful how to express the findings and images to the client. This meant I had to trust the words that were channelling through my mind, describing what my inner eyes witnessed.

The risk was that my client would believe me to be somewhat deluded and never return or worst case scenario, report me to the German board of Naturopathic doctors which yes, practise holistic medicine, but do not usually integrate psychic elements. They are very clinical and refer to giving injections or herbal remedies, so my technique was controversial and almost had to be kept a secret.

An elderly lady came to me suffering from a stiff neck and dizziness. After my initial examination I asked her to lie down on my treatment couch so I could begin with the medical examination and possible areas that link with her neck issues.

For this I would close my eyes and allow my hands to take over - I can see through my hands.

Luckily, a few years later one documentary explained that one can have retina cells in other parts of the body and also in the palms of the hand (I know...but it is true) It acts more like the third eye or inner eye, but nevertheless my hands can see and translate the information.

As I was gliding my hands down either side of her face something made me pause over her left cheek in particular. What I saw looked like half a metal screw, similar to what dentists use for tooth implants, but it was only the tip of the screw. As I continued scanning I could find nothing further and continued with the healing session.

When I finished I told her what I saw and asked if this was at all possible. She replied with: "No, this cannot be possible; I have been with the same dentist for 20 years and trust him completely." She did confirm having had a tooth implant treatment done several years back.
I advised her to get a scan so we can be sure all is well, and I may well be wrong.

She returned to me the following week and said her dentist refuses to do a scan and accused me of being a quack. "Ok", I said "we will not find out unless you have a scan done", so in the end she went to a different dentist for the scan. The results were as follows.

There was indeed one part of the implant which had somehow broken off and was stuck somewhere in her top gum, having developed into a plum sized puss filled cyst, which was the reason for her dizzy spells and the heart problem and palpitations, due to the fact that if tooth inflammations go on untreated with antibiotics the bacteria can settle on the heart valves and can cause severe damage gradually all over the body.

So with this information - my ability that I possess psychic vision, had been proven as correct, which in one way made me very happy, but also left me feeling slightly puzzled as to why and *how* I could see into people's bodies...well she was my first. She had to have the cyst and four teeth removed surgically and needed extensive work done to rebuild bone in her gums and after that had healed, four new implants.

I suggested that she should speak to her old dentist and take the current scan to her to show him and get his reply to the findings after calling me a quack and having lied to her. He was not very happy with the evidence and refused to explain himself nor did he offer to treat her or correct anything.

It continued to become increasingly hostile so I organised a lawyer for my client to prosecute him. The dental work was costing her a fortune, which she did not have and I am very much for justice. She suffered because he treated her with neglect and refused to correct his mistakes. Also she lost four further teeth because of him and contracted possible damage to her heart.

She was very frightened to continue with the court case but I assured her she will win and we stayed in touch.

Like everything when linked to legal matters, months went by and unfortunately, I moved from Germany to England before her case was completed, so I was unable to stand by her until the end.

A few months later I received a phone call from her and she had won the case and all was well. She was delighted and thanked me for possibly saving her life and for helping her develop the courage to stand up for her right.

I was very much moved and knew from that day forward to take my 'gift' very seriously.

Since then, I have had many unique experiences combining the healing with increasing visits from loved ones who have crossed over to the spirit world, especially over the last few years.

It seems that I was tuning into the same frequency that is used for channelling healing and creating a contact line for spirit.

I have gained insight into the energy 'Love' and know that this energy is the most powerful force in the entire Universe. It never disappears it just changes shape.

When we lose our physical body, we still remain linked to our loved ones and somehow have access to the data of who we were in our life time, almost like a unique print version on a CD-disk that will be there for eternity, (how long exactly I am unsure of).

Chapter Twenty-Two
My Relationship with Spirit

My relationship with Spirit

My first encounter with communication from Spirit began with the death of my very much-loved Grandma. Not one day passes, since her crossing that I do not communicate with her or think of her in some way throughout my day, not because I can`t get over her physical parting but I always felt somehow she is with me.

In my early days working with clients, if and when I would sense a loved one coming through, I was unsure whether to say something or not also because I did not trust what I was getting as information. I was very aware of the damage I could create, if I gave wrong information, which would leave me looking unprofessional.

So I found a Psychic College, which I visited for a year and a half in attempt to give me greater insight and understanding how to translate the images and information I received during communication with Spirit.

The Psychic College however I found was more like a playground for people who wanted to be psychic and were using or trying to use this ability to escape from planet earth or to be someone special to receive praise or even success by lying to people.

During my time in this group I found a couple of people out of 20 to be genuinely psychically gifted, at the beginning of their journey, just like myself.

The rest were as I would call lost with the fairies, ungrounded and somewhat deluded. I believe that this ability develops over time, even if you are born with it.

A few things you should know about psychics, and I am only speaking for myself here as I cannot speak for any others out there.

- I cannot predict the lottery.
- I too have bad days, which sometimes cloud the quality, of a reading.

Science tries to measure psychic evidence with applying in my opinion stupid guessing games using cards with symbols that have to be called out correctly by the psychic. If he or she fails to get this right, this apparently proves that they are a fraud or real.

This has nothing to do with communication to spirit and is a total waste of time. It will never prove anything. In my opinion the reason why it can`t work is due to fact that numbers and symbols are a dead energy and Mediums or Psychics connect to a type of energy that is very much alive. I certainly do.

What will be much more interesting is to connect the Psychic to an EEG - machine or maybe something even better in the years to come which would be able to highlight the areas of the brain that sparks up when connecting with spirit, which I am sure would be visible.

In my personal experience, I sense them coming into my thought system, mainly through the right side of my brain in the back of my head. Then it unfolds further as the connection becomes clearer.

My clients in particular know that I could not have known what I share with them, as I usually receive the contact with their first visit.

I also do not do what is called 'cold reading', which means one apparently searches for signs of confirmation within the persons facial features.

I am sure some or a lot out there do this, I don`t. Of course you will find a lot of dubious types out there but let`s be honest here, you find that in every profession offered on the planet.

I receive information as the client lies down and look to the side as I am trying to concentrate on the words or images coming in. Even more information enters in when I sit behind my client and touch their head, which I often do when applying healing techniques.

It varies. I also see their Aura colour and can read their body`s energy.
I use and integrate all of these techniques as part of the treatment. Each session is tailored to the needs of the client.

The results speak for themselves.

Remember unseen energy is unpredictable especially for me working on the other end of the line.

Each and every one of my clients is highly valued and I take my job very seriously.

Over the last months I have noticed a vast increase of interest in psychics and everything linked to the supernatural and life after death.

Only last week I saw a TV programme, featuring a story of a male scientist who had contracted the worse form of meningitis and ended up in a coma for some time. They thought he had a 2% chance of survival.

During his coma, and being observed by other doctors, later confirmed that he could not have experienced or seen what he did using a particular part of his brain which is said to create nice images for us when we cross over to make our passing a nicer experience, (a chemical shutdown response created by the brain.) because that part of the cortex was reported as dead.

He came out of the coma, fully conscious, which was a miracle in itself and reported that he had seen the Spirit world and recognised several people he knew who had crossed over. He described the Spirit world filled with luscious green plants, flowers, butterflies, stunning scenery and a beautiful bright light welcomed him and drenched him with a deep sense of love.

The reason for this particular story to be more believable than previous discoveries is due to the fact that he himself is a scientist, was a sceptic and the cortex of his brain was out of function during his coma so it could not produce images of fantasy.

He wrote a book, I think it is called: 'The Map of Heaven'. After-death experiences have been reported since time of Plato and have always been very similar.

What I personally found very interesting was that he spoke about the intense feelings of being surrounded by this amazing energy which is what I too have experienced, but in my meditation, not because I died.

It is this powerful all knowing, non judgemental invisible force energy 'Love' that I work with as a channel and I want everyone to get the chance to be able to release the old and negative and to reconnect to themselves and become complete and balanced again, so their life can continue on a much brighter path.

It is definitely there, but we need to make that first step and want to heal ourselves first from within and then the exterior world changes accordingly for us.

I do believe that we are experiencing a rise in energy awareness globally. Something is increasingly trying to get through to make sure that most of us change their negative thought systems into positive, why exactly, I am currently not sure, but I will keep you posted.

Wouldn't it be fantastic if we could exchange War, Greed & Ignorance for Love, Health and Happiness!

Chapter Twenty-three
My Unseen Friends

My unseen Friends

Returning to my personal experience with Spirit I would like to share with you some of my stories, linked to my healing work.

Case study one

A lady came to me, in need for some treatment to reduce stress and anxiety. As I do with every new client, I take notes listen to their story and begin to read into their energy as they share their story with me.

My reading was interrupted by a strong presence of a male energy, which was very clear in making his presence known to me and said who he was and how he was connected to the person sitting there. He said he passed very suddenly, which was confirmed by my client. He had passed with heart attack during a meal he and his friends were enjoying whilst out together in a restaurant.

He continued to describe his character to me, his hobbies, his love for music and playing the guitar and making other people happy, as many as possible which he did. He even repeated a sentence, word for word that he said a couple of weeks prior to his passing in front of my client, which she remembered. He continued to connect for almost an hour.
She was a sceptic before she came and I had no intention to give her a reading, but wanted to apply a healing treatment instead.

Sometimes they decide what`s best, they know better than I so I trust and go with the flow.

My client left feeling very deeply moved by this encounter and passed all the information on to her husband, who is a very close friend of the deceased.
She thanked me for opening her eyes.

I believe Spirit comes through for the individual seeking help but they too receive some form of healing and peace by communicating and finding short bursts of memory exchange.

I my experience they come through especially describing their character and personality aspects, which I believe to be very important for recognition and evidence.

Some have a clearer connection than others. I do not know why, but I assume it is due to their energy and also my ability to connect on the day.

Working as a healer I feel I need to pass on and do what I have been given and so if it is healing passed on by connecting to spirit, I shall continue to do so, if my clients are comfortable with that.

Case study two

Another lady came to see me for a reading a few weeks after losing her 30 year old daughter to cancer. Her daughter had to leave her little boy behind, like so many stories so tragic.

To make things even more difficult I had seen her daughter three weeks prior to her passing for some healing and we had an in depth conversation about her worries and fears, so I was aware of her concerns of having no choice but to leave her six year old son behind.

It was a first for me to try and create a spirit link, after I had a personal encounter and a bit of information from our previous conversation, so the evidence I would need was to receive information that I could not have received previously, which put me under even more pressure.

After a little while, her daughter did come through and first of all described her last day at the hospital and showed me how she was wheeled around in a wheelchair and had something blue, folded, placed into her lap. She explained that when she opened this card, it played a sound that was very special to her.
I could not have known this, as I was not in the hospital with her, only her mother was.

Having said those word her mother burst into tears and confirmed that the blue thing was a self-made song card, which when opened played back the voice of her little boy

Chills were shooting up and down my spine! Words cannot describe the feeling I receive when I am connected. I was overcome with the deep sense of love for her son

This was the only time I could feel a deep sense of sorrow from her. How awful the thought knowing you are dying and have to leave your child behind and in addition she did not want her ex-partner to see her son (which was of course very difficult to avoid by law).

I sense that even if we pass and lose the physical shell, our body, we continue to feel that deep love bond, how and where exactly I do not know yet. It seems to transcend over and across both worlds that is why I know Love is the strongest energy and overpowers all.

She then suddenly switched her attention to food. She showed me a huge plate of Spaghetti Bolognaise and she smiled, whilst sending me the image she was tucking in and absolutely loving it.

Her mother confirmed that was her favourite dish, but due to all the medication she was sick the entire time towards the end although she very much loved her food.

Her daughter came through so clearly that it was my honour to pass the information on to her grieving mother, to offer her the some form of connection line and the evidence that her daughter had safely transitioned into the spirit world.

She was happier when she left and visited me several times after, each time her daughter connected with updates and links to current situation her mother was in.

She said that this did help her to cope with the worst time and opened her eyes to a new form of relationship with her beloved daughter.
She was a very brave and special lady who had a deep sense wisdom and understanding. I admired her strength and grace.

Case study three
My next case relates to one of my male clients who suffered a traumatic fall from a tree at the age of seven, which left him completely deaf in his right ear.

I began with my healing. After 10 minutes I was interrupted by a male presence that described himself to be the father of my client.

He had died when my client was three years of age, and who is now 55, so he has waited a long time to connect. He admitted, that he was scared at first but then deeply touched and surprised by his father coming through.

His father held up a photo in his hand showing my client as a little boy sitting on his lap. I now know that this photo exists and is one of the only ones my client processes.

He showed me how he would rock his son on his knee and gave me awareness about a significance linked to the size of his hands being very big, which was also confirmed.

He then showed me the sea and a special connection with the army, and how proud he was to have been part of it, so much so that he enlisted twice. He also appeared in army clothing.

All of this may not sound much, but for my client it was all he needed and he was delighted and moved to tears.

I felt deeply honoured to be part of this moment, because each time I can feel that huge sense of overwhelming love in the entire room, permeating through my client and me.

It is truly magical and even slightly addictive for me to be part of it and also to have been chosen to perform such a special and lovely type of work.

My client has not been the same since this encounter...He has since had three healing sessions and is currently experiencing healing sensations in his ear, and has regained some of his earing for the first time since he was seven.

His Testimonial:

"I have only known Britta for a short time but the time I have spent with her has completely changed my perspective on life and my understanding of the importance of loving yourself in terms of the positive effect this can have on your mind body and spirit. Britta is a gentle soul who listens carefully before sharing her wisdom and healing powers.

Along with her wisdom comes intricate knowledge of the body and mind and the Universe, which she is able to channel and use to help you to recharge and restore your zest for life. As a result of her treatments I feel that I am in charge of my own destiny and I have a bright, interesting and loving future ahead."

Case study four

I also saw a lady who came to me with several physical issues but most were related as I found out later due to her experience a chain of traumatic events the most intense being the loss of her daughter to bowel cancer.

I very often ask for clients to bring photos of the person they want to connect to as this helps with the connection and adds to the flow of information. She brought a photo of a group gathering on a summer afternoon and immediately her daughter pointed out to me where she was in the picture.

She began to describe briefly how she felt in her last days of earthly life, her character and also that she had to leave her little daughter behind.

She confirmed she was a strong willed lady who would not hesitate to speak her mind if she did not like you.

She then added that she was not happy with the male who was looking after her daughter, which I remember to be her ex-husband, who had since re married. She came through with such clarity and detail, that her mother recognised all and was much more at peace after her connection.

None of the readings will ever bring back your loved ones but I believe to know that they are ok and around in such detail can be a very healing experience and help us to move forward to focus more on our path until we meet again.

In my experience a lot of my clients have found the connections a support in their grieving process, and that to me is a form of healing too.

Our loved ones do not want us to continue to put our life on hold for longer than necessary, they are ok and want us to be happy again.

Some clients grieve for 10 years or more and yes, on a certain level we never get over the loss, but we must find a way to adapt to the changes and day by day, step by step, emerge and remember that we are still in that physical body, needing to continue our learning journey.

Case study five
Another time I saw a lady who came to me for stress releasing and healing. During my healing I suddenly saw a head of a horse appear right in front of me. It was beautiful, white and came through with such Love for the owner.

With the appearance of the horse, my client's gate for emotional release was opened and she began to tell me her story, sobbing and I almost with her. It proves a difficult task at times to stay in that healing distance with all the stories that are presented to me.

This horse was very loved by my client and it suddenly became ill and she had to let the vet come to end its life and she spoke to it whilst the vet ended its pain with the fatal injection. The horse was showing me images and gave impressions of the calm it felt and all was ok. You cannot imagine what this message meant to my client.

For years she had been riddled with feelings of guilt if she had done the right thing or if there was anything else she could have done to save her beloved animal.

Yes we can love animals just as much and they too stay around in this love connection energy too.
My clients stress slowly diminished after this encounter. She released all those suppressed tears held deep within for many years.

Often people do not give our animal friends enough credit or assume they do not have emotions, of course they have they just express them in a different way and less complex, which does not mean they do not have emotions.

Some animals are of a higher intelligence frequency then others but we meet the right ones for us and they are very often our silent helper who sooth our burden and brighten our daily lives.

I have a deep respect for this pure form of unconditional love and we can sometimes learn a lot from our furry friends.

In some cases when Spirit came through they too show which animal they are looking after and very often it is either a dog or a cat whichever animal was part of their past and had died.

They often show me beautiful fields of green where they allow their dogs to run and play freely or by the sea.

They can go wherever they choose in a split second.
Being no longer in the physical body makes this possible. They experience a total different awareness of time and own an ability to jump in between years as if it is a second.

Case study six
Another of my lovely male clients came to me to reduce stress levels. He was very much interested about learning the concept of positive thought and so the focus was to perform a few sessions introducing whilst removing stress patterns out of his system.

However, as soon as I began to place my hands on either side of his head, his father came through with a very mischievous character and focused on his son's love for cars and that he was aware his son was going to purchase a new one in the colour blue, to my client's amazement.

His mother followed shortly after, and presented me not only with the image of a baking tray covered in very lovely homemade warm biscuits, but I could also smell them and it made me salivate.

This made both of us laugh and my client remembered what a great cook his mother was. Furthermore she then told me that her son still eats sweets and chocolates and biscuits in secret - and too much of them! Again, we had to laugh.

It felt as if she was in the room with us chatting, very amused about revealing her sons secrets. She then showed me the interior of her living room furniture where her son grew up and was busy swinging her dusting cloth as she loved everything to be sparkly clean.

She had such a lovely energy, both his parents have. It feels as if they are at peace with where they are and they were very aware of their son`s activities.

My client is a very intuitive person, which I may say at this stage that men often do not get chance to express this side, even though they are.

He has returned for regular sessions due to the positive programming plan and enjoys each treatment.

The most recent encounter was very interesting due to a slight change in my reading. What I picked up on that particular session was something showed me the name 'Mason'.

I asked him to define the term used and he did. I continued with the healing but was soon interrupted by an image of him in a previous life, hastily walking through the tiny alleys in a village called Manningtree. I have not heard of this area before, neither was I aware of the fact that people practised witch hunting there. The next image given to me was a pub called Fox and…something. I could not see the missing name underneath. In addition I was shown that he and a few other men would meet up in this pub to discuss how to gather the women they had found. That was all.

After the session I scribbled a quick sketch on what I saw him wearing and we decided to find out if this pub ever existed.

To our 'surprise' not only does the pub still exist but it was also the meeting point for witch hunters in the time period I saw. He was mortified to have been part in such activity, as he is the kindest man with the biggest heart in this life.

I know most of us have killed in previous lives, if for survival and most of all due to the fact that a life was not worth much.

We were speechless. This was the first time that I have ever received information from a living energy linking to a possible past life and found confirmation.

I thought I would share this little story with you...

Another very special encounter is when a child comes through especially when it has barely touched the earth plane.

Case study seven
Another lady came to see me with tension in her upper back and a little Irritable Bowel Syndrome (IBS) symptoms and tension in her stomach area.

As I was reading her body and my hands were above her pelvic area, I was suddenly flooded with goose bumps, which always tells me that a very high frequency is present, almost angelic.
My client had her eyes closed and suddenly the entire energy in my practise room changed. The temperature dropped.

Everything was drenched a subtle pink in my mind`s eye and I received a very strong impression of the presence of a little baby girl. I had no knowledge of my clients past and the fact that she had lost her.

With the energy of the girl getting increasingly stronger, I heard myself say: "Have you lost a girl?" Simultaneously my client burst out saying the words: "Oh my god I have just seen my daughter. Her face came really close over mine and she hovered and said I am ok and I love you mummy."

Words cannot describe the energy present in my practise in this moment.

The energy was so pure and so full of Love that it felt like being embraced by an angel.

For several minutes we were both stunned and after the energy evaporated we were able to exchange the story of my clients past.

There was a lot of residual heartache and guilt and uncertainty in connection with the loss of her baby girl.

This encounter changed my client`s life and she finally found peace. That feeling is the greatest gift of all.

Sometimes when we ask for healing we can be surprised by how the Universe chooses to help to set us free.

All those precious moments that I get to share with my clients who open up and trust my abilities, is the reason that has made my journey to the point where I am today, having overcome many obstacles.

I have grown together over the last years with my client`s stories and our joint experiences.

I learn every day and am very grateful for this opportunity.

Chapter Twenty-Four
My Story

My Story

I was born several weeks early, in North Germany, a small town by the name Schleswig- Holstein. As if I could not wait to begin my earthly journey.

Until the age of three we lived in Schleswig, but then moved to Düsseldorf, a big city more towards the South.

My father was a Lithographer and started to work in a bigger firm with the main focus on advertisement. He is also a Jazz musician (Dixie-jazz), plays guitar and the banjo. The Jazz scene was very big in Düsseldorf in the 70`s.

My mother was busy handling a household and two girls and keeping everything in balance.

I would say that I was always sensitive to picking up on moods and energy, which began to become more noticeable to me and everyone else, from the age of seven. I used to suffer from bad dreams, always scenes from the war and me dying in it, either suffocating from gas or getting shot.

No one really spoke that much about it and I accepted it as being part of me.

As a child one does not question visions, dreams etc. as we do later in life as adults, we just accept and live with it.

Overall everything was in balance until the age of six, when my school year began. I was born with a high level of sensitivity and for some reason always was accompanied by a sense of tension and fear, not so much when back at home or when playing outside with my childhood friend Stephen, who very often suffered under the consequences of my leadership quality in our games.

We used to meet up every day and play in our local park nearby. We used to enjoy a variety of role-play games ranging from detectives to pirates and loved to race using his go-cart. I would stand up behind grabbing onto his shoulders and he had to pedal as fast as he could. We would take turns and time would just fly by.

That is also how I missed my first official school day.

Prior to the first school day, mothers bring their children and one gets introduced to the head teacher and class teacher and receives a triangular paper- school bag full of gifts, sweets etc. That would be the nicest part of this ritual for me.

My class teacher unfortunately was a German lady in her 50s at the time, ancient to me, and always screamed everything she tried to communicate to us pupils instead of talking in a normal voice.

All the teachers seemed to suffer from halitosis (very smelly breath) and each time one of them would bend down to communicate I had to hold my breath so I would not pass out.

However, far worse was my male teacher Dr Frank. He should have been called Dr Frankenstein, he was just evil and loved to humiliate and pick on vulnerable children - ie.me!

In general, certain subjects that did not interest me in the slightest would force me to gaze out of the class room window, due to much more important things causing distraction...birds...trees and what to play after school with Stephen. Or I would scribble whilst really trying to listen.

For some reason he had decided to pick on me for a long time and began to humiliate me in front of the class by making me read something, which he knew I was not good at due to my nerves.

He would stop me after my face was almost exploding with blushing. He would say: "You are stupid, aren't you?" "Say that you are stupid!" "Out loud, so everyone can hear it."

"Tell the class how stupid you are. So I did, and was rewarded with roaring laughter.

That was the start of being bullied and with each day my confidence began to waste away. Each morning walking to school I would already experience the embarrassment and hatred I felt towards Dr Frank!

I had to suffer under him for a few years and at the end of the school term before one changes school again to the next school, he called the parents, in my case my mother to confirm that I am a hopeless case and will not be good enough to visit a Gymnasium, which is for the brainy ones.

I did pay him a visit at a later stage when I was a teenager and expressed my feelings towards him as person and how he failed on every level. It did make me feel a lot more at peace in myself.

My happiest memories looking back at my childhood overall were the summer school holidays, my sister and I would spend with my favourite Grandmother in her Cottage in Schleswig. She was my mother's mum and she was very unique. She was my rock, my strength and by far the best cook on the planet.

Backing on to her garden was a vegetable plot, which she had lovingly planted, overflowing with endless variety of vegetables and fruits: beans, carrots, potatoes, cabbages, strawberries, black currants, apples, pears etc.

She cooked everything in the old way, with butter and each meal was prepared with such effort and love, and very rich in fat.
She baked the juiciest cakes, created the yummiest puddings and she owned a food chamber cabinet in her tiny kitchen that was always filled with anything and everything us children but also the grownups could nibble at any time we fancied, well kind of. The taste still lingers with me, after 30 years of her passing.

She was a strong-minded character and what you saw was what you got. Very often people say I am very similar and even look a lot like her. If that is the case I am very proud.
I will be forever grateful to her for so many things.

She had encountered so many awful situations during the war; she suffered a lot under the Russians who raped every girl, no matter the age. They used to make them stand in a circle and pick out the next victims.

She also travelled in an attempt to escape, sitting on explosives hiding in Lorries, which could have blown up at any stage. She always refused to carry out the Hitler greeting everyone was forced to do. She was very brave lady and tried to protect others and keep them safe. On top of all that, her own health was in danger several times and she almost died twice due to deadly viruses but somehow made it through it all and always remained kind with an open heart for others.

I have the deepest respect for her and all the individuals who survived the horrors of war, the starving, the constant fear and terror, the loss, I do not know how they coped and how most of them found a way to come back to everyday life.
They were of a special genetic design.

Often I wish my Grandmother would still be here physically and I could pop over to visit her and exchange conversation and absorb her wisdom and of course enjoy her amazing cooking abilities.
She was able to talk away warts and seemed to own healing abilities. I regret deeply never really finding out more during her lifetime, but I was too small and later very self absorbed in my negativity and she never spoke about it to me. I do miss the purity and simplicity of those days when everything tasted better, was cleaner, not so polluted and overcrowded.

My sister and I would share many happy summer beach days with my Grandmother and she always did something that made us laugh. We both absolutely loved our holidays. She passed to the Spirit world when I was 18 years old.

It was from that day I became aware of spirit and the deeper healing abilities. Maybe she passed it down to me. I believe she did.

As a child I had a natural aptitude for drawing & painting and music that was never encouraged. Everything was much more private and part of daily life and not looked into any further. Everyone was more occupied with his or her daily lives.

Looking back I believe I could have expanded my talent but the exterior world and media made sure that my belief system in relying that one could earn money with art or music was an unfulfilled fantasy and would only be possible as a hobby when one has a proper job earning money.

Overall I did not see that much of my father, and most of the time when he would come home from work one was not allowed to greet him with loud enthusiasm or make much noise. Sitting at the dining table one strict glare was enough to reassure me to sit up in perfect posture and eat without chewing sounds and not speak and definitely not laugh.

It was a difficult task to fulfil when one is a small person, overflowing with energy and happy to see ones father even when somewhat grumpy almost on a daily basis.
All I wanted was to please my father and to be loved. I tried everything and sometimes made him laugh. I was a positive attention seeker, I made sure I was always thinking of new ideas that would make him see that I was special, talented and he could be proud of me.

At the age of six I fitted into my fathers banjo case and was always very proud to carry it for him to his gigs. It made me feel as if I was famous.

The happiest memories I have with my father I would say link to the Jazz- music events and all the characters one would meet there. The atmosphere was always rather jolly, probably due to the large amount of beer infusions. We once went fishing together, just the two of us. What I did love was to hold his hand when I walked next to him on occasion asking him about anything and everything. I could sense his gentle and somewhat suppressed loving aspects, flowing from his hand into mine.

I will never forget the softness of his hands or smell. I believe most of us recognise our parent`s unique scent especially when we are little. I used to love my father`s aroma of old spice lingering in his shirts. Just a sniff and I felt safer.

I learnt to play the classical music on the piano at the age of nine and was part of a choir for a while. I loved to sing but would have never had the courage to sing in public.

The piano playing and learning to read notes was very difficult for me but I did it for a while. I was more scared of my piano teacher then able to enjoy my hobby. Germans are too strict.

By the age of 11, I had to take the tram to my new school now, which was always ram packed with people, coughing, passing wind or other unpleasant aspects that one was forced to endure on a daily basis.

This new school was even worse for me as I was terrified of my maths teacher who would always force me to solve the unsolvable on the black board to the amusement of all the others.

In addition unfortunately, my father decided to leave us for another woman who he had been seeing behind my mother`s back for only two years! Sensitivity was not his forte.

Initially, it was almost a relief because my parents would have had terrible arguments and he would sometimes get physical towards my mother. The tension and negative atmosphere used to make me ill, almost once a month. My only concern was if I could visit him in his flat and heard the word "yes", so I was at ease for the moment not having been rejected. It sucks being smaller and feeling helpless. I know now it was the only way my body was trying to escape and find new strength from somewhere.

The emotional turmoil of my father leaving were beginning to have an negative effect on me and I became even worse and sank to my lowest abilities at school so they decided to place me in one of the roughest institutions, where the drop outs go or the younger teens from families with alcohol abuse etc. - ideal for me I thought.

This was an entire different ball game. Fear and terror took over, reason being I was bullied every day. They would hunt me down at break time and jam my hand in toilet doors and threatened to beat me up or strip me naked in front of the rest of the class.

They would get hold of my ponytail and threaten to chop all my hair of whilst armed with huge scissors. They would grab me at break time and chuck me into the huge outdoor bins.
I knew their words had meaning as they performed several unkind rituals to others every morning. Teachers were absolutely useless and helpless, so they did not try and teach anything. I was on my own as usual.

Every day was a nightmare for me and any strategy I tried to either stay invisible, never make eye contact and be very friendly all proved futile. In the end it got so bad that I decided not to go back. I pretend to my mother go to school and just walked aimlessly in our park or hang around until the time would come to get back home. All in all I managed to keep up the facade for 14 days, and then my mother received a telephone call from the school, enquiring if I was sick.

I had to explain what I have been experiencing and my mother rang two of the worst pupils, which I believed would seal my certain death when I had to face them.

Of course they would be friendly on the phone! Any child who has experienced being bullied will know that this would be the worst thing to do. However I ended up standing in front of my entire class explaining why I had been skiving! By that time I was beyond caring what would happen to me. I resigned to my fate.

Luckily, by that time we were only a few more weeks away from moving to England, and that idea seemed a welcomed relief.

Bizarrely, since my talk in front of the class all the girl bullies were now suddenly transformed into my personal bodyguards and hovered around me the entire time making sure I stayed unharmed, but they just chose someone else to pick on.

Not really sure what the lesson was here...

By the age of 11, I was convinced that I would never understand numbers mathematics or history etc. and always remembered that I was stupid anyway, so I closed off.

Homework was torture for me. Unfortunately my mother did not own much patience and would often express her frustration, by screaming at me, which of course was just going to thicken the plank of wood in front of my head.

Outwardly I appeared to be tough, but on the inside it was a different matter. I felt a sense of responsibility to look after my mum.

My sister went through a phase of never being at home and so I was left with my mother who was grieving and not coping very well with the separation.

It was a dark time and turned even darker when I was sexually abused at the age of 11. Some deluded and disturbed man decided to choose me to experience feelings of dread and disgust, which would strongly mark my views and opinions of the male race.

As many of you know in the 70`s one was aware of sexual abuse but everything was kept hidden or hushed, nothing like today.

I decided to keep it a secret from my father and everyone else. I won`t go into details as it does not matter anymore, but it was not a confidence boost for my already sensitive and stupid ego.

It seemed that somehow since that encounter I would attract all sorts of weird moments, for example standing in a jam packed tram men would stand up close to me rubbing their genitals against me, an act concealed by the crowd.

My friend, Stephen and I went to a cinema I had a man who was masturbating sitting next to my and he another girl to his left. He was very busy looking from side to side, but unfortunately I was too stunned to move. All I managed to whisper was: "Stephen that man next to me is masturbating." We just stayed and pretended not to see.

Those were the days. My world seemed to be filled with those types of encounters and my father was no support what so ever, so I developed a lot of aggression towards men altogether.

I had no idea that this would follow me for years and create negative attraction. If I would have had the knowledge of today I probably could have spared myself one lesson or two.

By the age of 15 my mother and I moved to England because she had met and fallen in love with an English man. We lived in the middle of nowhere and the transition from German school system to the English school system was anything but easy for me.

I will never forget the moments when I sat in the head teachers` office waiting to be walked to my class, the only German girl in a school full of English strangers. At that time my English was not much more than "hello my name is" and "thank you." I was numb with fear awaiting my new destiny. I hated to have to wear skirts and tights, as we in Germany wear what we want. I always thought that the idea that wearing school uniform would stop people noticing who had more or less money was absolute rubbish. You could see a mile off if someone's skirt or trousers were tacky, too short, too baggy or simply knackered.

That concept was one of the many challenges I faced living in the United Kingdom.

Within several days the other pupils surrounded me like a precious prey and they bombarded me with questions. The boys liked me but most of the girls hated me.

I developed a sexual interested in boys but felt very ugly, which I found confirmed when looking into the mirror. Spots and a metal brace would stare back at me, and I was skinny and flat chested a nightmare for a teenage girl. All the other English girls had bras, something we did not have in Germany for teenagers.

What I found even more puzzling was that even though I was so ugly, boys would still fancy me.

I was a walking cocktail of defensiveness and lacking confidence, and absolutely obsessed by my attempts to make me look better. My endless inner craving for acceptance and love, praise or something positive made me say yes which should have been no`s and just added to my inner war of feeling not good enough and unattractive and stupid.

At the age of 17-18 I left England under great difficulty, because I felt emotionally deeply connected to England, but due to nothing being available work wise for me at that time and my father`s request to share my talent for art by becoming a Lithographer as he was - I agreed.

My father assured me that a vacancy in his firm was available for me to join him as a lithographer, which would be the ideal job for someone who is creative, artistic, so he said.

Little did I know what was waiting for me, back home in Germany

His new wife was a bit cold natured, a teacher and alternative, which may not mean much to you but we translate alternative as no warmth, no spice, expressing of a bland nature and wearing clogs, no make-up etc. She also had bad cooking skills and the house felt cold most of the time.

I had not quite unpacked my suitcase and was heavily exhausted from the long journey when she approached me with the words: "You can keep the first wage", meaning one month, and after I would have to pay half my wages to live there. For the room I stayed in and apparently the electric I'd be using up.

My first wage was round about 350 so half was already taken and I had not even started with the apprenticeship. I felt very unwelcome, and wished I had stayed in England, but it was too late and I never give up before having tried my best.

My eyes searched for support from my father but he just looked to the floor in silence. My room was very small and pretty cold, just like everything in that household.

My apprenticeship was set up for three years, which is expected in Germany; otherwise you do not qualify in any profession. Every six weeks one has to visit a school, which accompanies the development in chosen profession, but also requires mathematics, physics and many others, which I dreaded.

Here we go again I thought, it felt like my death sentence.

My experience in the firm was very intense too. It was always very tense due to the tight time schedule to get the film material ready to send off for printing, and then receive a pre - print to correct minor faults in colouring.

For example if I had to make someone's eye 'white' bluer if it was too yellow or red.

It was these corrections, which were very complicated, and one had to have an excellent eye for precision and detail and make decisions in seconds, which would either be a failure or success. If a bigger mistake was made, the client would not pay the amount and the one who worked on it would experience hell on earth. This happened rarely but pressure was on from the moment one walked through the door until leaving totally exhausted.

At times when we did catalogues we sometimes worked 12 hours flat and all the time hovering above a table which was lit up from underneath, effecting your eyes. Cutting 'masks' with the use of a sharp scalpel was my main task and a boss - a psycho - who again chose me to scream at most of the day.

I never received back up or support from my father, he just observed. I did get the impression that he did not like any confrontation so just left it all to me and also because he didn't really care. Maybe he thought this would toughen me up.

For me every day was hell and I began developed many stress linked physical imbalances, like allergies where I would be covered in hives and one time my tongue swelled up so much I had to go for a steroid injection so I would not suffocate. I just could not cope with all the negativity. I began to visit a variety of doctors who all confirmed I had stress.

After several time wasting visits to a variety of specialists, it was beginning to wind me up and I felt brushed off, no one actually took anything I said to heart or would help me.

Words often used: "you are just too sensitive".
This seemed to be the answer to it all, my curse. Was it really that bad to be sensitive? I was convinced that I was the problem at that time. I took that as another addition to my many negatives.
Being sensitive was a weakness, something else to dislike in myself.

During this time I used to fly back and forth to England to visit my mother and my sister, in my holidays, my sister had also moved to England because she found love.

I survived my time in the firm but had more frequent arguments with my stepmother, who by now was mother to my stepbrother. She was very busy applying stickers with commands: for example, a sticker was placed on the tap saying: "tighten me properly after use." In the refrigerator more stickers on tomatoes, saying: "you can`t eat me, I have to wait until Saturday."

Overall very unpleasant and I was still paying for...not exactly sure? I began to get increasingly angry and rebellious by age 19 and confronted her. In addition she decided to sleep with my baby stepbrother outside my bedroom door as he screamed 24/7.

I was approaching the end phase of my apprenticeship and had to get up at 5am for school so sleep was very precious to me. It was all too hostile for me and I would have become physically violent towards her, had I not left that house.

I ended up moving out and had to cope with living in a tiny smelly flat with hardly any money, again my father would have paid for a set of tyres if I had decided to drive a Citroën. I hated Citroën and drove Golf so I got nothing!

During this time I entered my first long term relationship of 11 years. Unfortunately he too had a very difficult mother and was her only son.

I gained further insight into rejection, never being good enough etc.

It seemed wherever I went and whatever I did, or whoever was in my nearest circle of relationship was somehow psychotic or extremely emotionally imbalanced, and every step was made as hard as it could be. Nothing was ever given freely or given with love.

By this time my confidence and self esteem hit its all time low and I began to develop behaviour of body dismorphia. This disorder is presented by an obsessive, constant need to negatively highlight physical appearance and body areas that are seem unbearably ugly and distorted and must be altered in order to continue daily life.

In those times all one could do was to purchase cosmetic products. There was no 'Botox' or 'Radio frequency-skin treatment' or 'laser skin renewal treatments' and even if they were available I would not have had the money to have anything done. Maybe it was just as well.
Not one day would pass without me picking on one or several parts of my face or body.

My nose was too long, too pointed, my teeth uneven, my skin too spotty, my body too skinny, my breasts too flat etcetera.

I felt so ugly, that for five years I refused to go to the beach in the summer, with the other young people or friends, so I would not have to get undressed or go swimming to spare others and myself the ugly view.

My poor partner tried his upmost best for years to make me open my eyes to my beauty. He was so patient and very kind to me, but I stayed in a dark place and was never able to see my beauty or love myself. Because I felt none for myself, as there was nothing unfortunately I was unable to give him any love too.

The constant struggle and feeling of being unwell or in pain brought my attention more and more into maybe finding answers and truth as to why I and others for that matter were experiencing physical imbalances linked to emotional imbalances.

I knew that there must be a way to discover an explanation or to find a solution and healing of some sort, rather than always being told it is stress, given pills to numb the symptoms for a while only to watch them grow even bigger never healed or understood.

I wanted to go to a medical school, for Naturopaths, a holistic approach to medicine, but nevertheless very demanding in knowledge of anatomy, physiology, pathology, psychology etc.

German authorities, reminded me, that my entire collection of Certificates, from England were unacceptable, and by far not enough to ever be allowed onto the German medical school for Naturopaths. I would either have to visit another school for further two years to repeat mathematics and many other subjects yet again that I had just completed in the school for lithographers for three years.

For 17 years I had tolerated various schools getting nowhere. Now I was rejected again and almost confirmed to be too stupid to ever attend the school for Naturopaths - the one thing I felt drawn to for once. I was absolutely livid, furious, beside myself! Surely something was going to be good enough at some stage?

Long story short it was the certificate from my time spent at the school for Lithographers, in Germany with seven passed subjects that enabled my entry into the medical school.

Finally! I was accepted and began with the intense medical courses, several evenings a week, all based in Latin, written and spoken language and German, alongside working for my partner's mother in her boutique during the daytime.

During the first year in my naturopath school, I felt our relationship had come to an end. I felt more sisterly towards someone I should have felt different about and I had to make a decision that I could not continue living with him and grow old together and have children, especially under the constant tyranny of his dominant and jealous, never satisfied mother.

We shared a house on separate floors, and I was no longer prepared to be screamed at or witness to endless arguments between her and my partner. It was all far too toxic. Stress always affected my immune system badly and I was more unwell then not.

We did part but stayed living together for two years after as friends, we always respected each other and he was a very important friend in my life and the only man I trusted. I am unsure if I would have made it during my times of study to become a Naturopath without him.

In addition to enable me to become the best I could be, I attended several classes and special groups to ensure the highest learning quality and intensity. I received Notification by the Board of Holistic Medicine who deferred my exam date from October to May, which meant that I lost several months of time to learn and prepare for this difficult and important exam.

In addition I was informed that out of 10 only one would pass because they are so strict and most of the women would fail.

Luckily they informed me during my most rebellious time and I was convinced I would show them if it was the last thing I would do.

It was one of the hardest things I had to do cope with mentally and physically. In special preparation for this exam I would get up at 5am, go straight into a specific topic then sleep for 30min or walk for 10 and continue all day every day for several months.

The first four weeks were hell. I felt as if my brain was going to burst under the pressure of information and the complexity. I suffered severe headaches and cried many days and night, but after the first month it changed to the opposite. I had tasted blood and was on fire, sucking information in like a hoover, and enjoying what I was learning for the first time in my life. I passed!

Soon after, I met my last partner with whom I shared a relationship for 13 years. I will not go into details here. Let's just say it was intense and looking at it positively I learnt a lot and loved him very much.

During our first two years being together, we came over to live in England in 2001 for various reasons. He was the owner of an estate agency and I ran a ladies fashion- boutique, first of all as a silent partner whilst completing my diploma in Progressive Kinesiology and Reiki and other courses.

Originally I was meant to stay a silent partner in the ladies fashion business, which my partner bought, but my so called friend at the time, whom we had both trusted, who worked in our joint boutique as our manager with other ladies as staff, had stolen money and my partner confronted her. Her reply was to leave along with most of the other staff. This meant I had to stop everything I was doing.

I had to find new staff and familiarise myself with: managing a boutique. Engaging with the fashion industry, learning to sell and communicate with people.
For me a nightmare, but I had no choice. One lady stayed with me for three weeks to help me a little and then she had to leave.

I was on my own and had to find staff. I ended up being successful and began to hope all would be fine soon and I could at least for several days in the week follow my true profession.

Six weeks into me taking over the boutique, someone set fire to my shop. The manager who at the time was living in the White Hart Hotel saved the building. My partner was called out the next morning and returned to me saying that I need to be strong because there had been a fire. I thought he was joking.

I followed him and as he stood in tears, which was twice in 13 years, I swore I would get the business back up and better than before.

In one second I gave away all I had learnt to become a practising Naturopath and Kinesiologist and put it all on hold.

At the time we owned the shop next door to the burnt boutique and working tirelessly for four weeks, I reopened my new shop with a window display that featured a fireman's uniform.

The clothing that was damaged by the fire was also not insured due to another unreliable person who worked for my partner, which added to the stress of trying to get the red figures back to black. To cut a long story short I did and the shop was a success.

The years of nonstop stress and no holiday and me developing endometriosis stage 3, brought me back to Germany for emergency surgery after being wrongly diagnosed by some useless English GP.

I ended up with two emergency operations by the age of 40, due to the severity and advanced stage adhesions causing me to pass out or collapse regularly in absolute agony. My bowels were badly affected and I was deeply exhausted.

I had no understanding at that time how it was all connected to my life, my relationships and my lack of self-love.

After 13 years my partner returned to Germany and I stayed in England. Just prior to that I had come to the conclusion that I must begin to focus on what I was born to do and I had put it all on hold for much too long, so I sold the boutique, using a technique from the law of attraction and then began with my deepest emotional make over and as I like to call it lovingly 'exorcism'.

It took me three years to release, and as I did most of my childhood experiences also decided to surface and required a lot of attention to detail, in order to be able to heal for good.

Reflecting back and revisiting my past, even if just for a brief moment, feels as if I wrote about someone else's life and darker days. Today, I know that most of my experiences were a result of me attracting them and they were there to enhance my knowledge or wisdom to help others who come and seek my help. How else would I be able to access the depth of being if my past spared me?

I am at peace with myself and love myself, which I thought impossible.

I am proud of my achievements so far and have grown immensely which I am truly grateful for.

The most important aspect when learning a lesson is not the suffering, but how we deal with it and how we come out the other side.

I hope both my book and my story have inspired you.
I want to thank all the individuals who have entered or touched my life and made this book possible.

My most important lesson was to learn to love myself, which I want to pass on to all of you. You are all unique and beautiful; you just need to wake up to it.

Sometimes the lessons seem endless but it is us who create what we experience!

You too have the power to change it. **Start today!**

Printed in Great Britain
by Amazon.co.uk, Ltd.,
Marston Gate.